Death and Life

Death and Life

Paul Fairfield

Algora Publishing
New York

Algora Publishing, New York
© 2001 by Algora Publishing
All rights reserved. Published 2001.
Printed in the United States of America
ISBN: 1-892941-72-4
Editors@algora.com

Library of Congress Cataloging-in-Publication Data 2001-004693

Fairfield, Paul, 1966-
  Death and life / by Paul Fairfield.
    p. cm.
  ISBN 1-892941-72-4 (alk. paper)
  1. Death. I. Title.
  BD444 .F29 2001
  128'.5—dc21
                              2001004693

New York
www.algora.com

Contents

PREFACE

Authors of books such as this one frequently write less than everything they think regarding their subjects. Scholarly writers, of which I am one, are especially inclined to play their cards close to the vest, whether so as not to be thought an extremist or to protect themselves from other criticism. It is part of every academic's training to learn to stick one's neck out only when necessary, which, according to most academic authors, is not often at all.

In writing this book, I have chosen to disregard this convention and instead to express as directly and straightforwardly as possible everything that I know, believe, or even suspect about my subject. That subject is nothing less than human life and death. Perhaps the topic is simply too important, to us all, for anyone writing about it to treat it as a mere curiosity or yet another academic puzzle in need of a solution. It seemed to me that death, in particular, and the experiences connected with it, was simply too serious a subject to be treated in the usual fashion, and that what was called for was a treatment that prized honesty over caution.

It seemed as well that because death and life are of ultimate importance to all human beings, it would be appropriate to address this book to a general reading audience rather than to one of profes- sional academics only. While the book is of a philosophical nature, it is not written (or not primarily) for an audience of specialists in philosophy, nor does it presuppose acquaintance with that field. For this reason, I have chosen to forego the technical language and niceties of scholarly writing and to express myself as straightfor- wardly as possible (or as is still possible for one accustomed to writing for an academic audience).

I have written this book on the conviction that an honest con- templation of death provides us with a perspective on life — human existence — that cannot be had by any other means. To understand anything is to do so from a definite perspective. Understanding hu- man life itself and its ultimate significance is notoriously difficult, but it is made easier if we approach it from an appropriate stand- point and with an appropriate set of questions. This standpoint, I would suggest, is what I have called (in the title of Chapter 1) "the encounter with death." This phrase refers equally to the experiences of dying, confronting one's mortality, and grieving the loss of an- other.

Contemplating these experiences serves several aims. The first is to comprehend in the most fundamental way the significance of these universal human experiences — and, by this means, to gain some insight into what makes peaceful resolution and acceptance possible. Second, reflecting on death provides a perspective on what would appear to be death's antithesis: life. If "the meaning of life" is too unwieldy a subject to be approached directly, perhaps the meaning of death provides an indirect route to the same end. Finally, while philosophical writing often serves practical ends, it also aims to understand the human condition for its own sake, and in a fashion that is as subtle and complex as its subject demands. When that subject is of no little complexity — as in this instance it most certainly is — an understanding of it must be equal in complexity; however, I have sought to do justice to the subtlety and complexity of the topic of this book without turning it into an academic exercise.

I have also written this book on the conviction that the prophetic words of Fyodor Dostoyevsky — that "we have all lost touch with life" — are true, and that the truth that they express is of considerable importance. Dostoyevsky expressed that observation well over a century ago, but when we contemplate the various elements of modern life, can we honestly declare it any less true at the present time than at the time it was made? How often do we hear the complaint not so much that we are unhappy, but that our lives lack something — something that we find difficult to describe, but that can be loosely captured in the word "meaning" or "ultimate significance"? It is as if some vital connection to life itself has been lost — but how are we to understand this, and how did it come to pass? Exactly what is it with which we have lost touch, and what possible remedy might we identify?

These are philosophical questions, but at the same time they are urgently practical questions to which modern culture almost frantically searches for an answer. A trip to most any bookstore reveals that what we anxiously desire are big answers to big questions — the old answers (as provided by the great world religions in particular) appearing to have lost their capacity to convince. This book does not offer new answers to ancient questions, but asks a series of questions relating to Dostoyevsky's observation and to the phenomenon of death. These are "existential" questions, or questions arising from the fundamental experience of being human: what is the meaning of death? What is it to "come to terms" with death, or indeed with life? Why is it that we turn our backs on death, preferring not to speak of it at all, much less to confront it directly? Do we not similarly turn our backs on life? Precisely what is it with which modern life has lost touch, and what alternative to this condition might there be?

Several of the observations and ideas that follow are drawn from a group of authors of the late nineteenth and early twentieth centuries known as "existential" philosophers, as well as from such figures as Dostoyevsky, Leo Tolstoy, Sigmund Freud, and others. Where appropriate, I have referred to or directly quoted numerous authors whose understanding of a certain point seems to me correct. As with many books of this nature, it attempts to synthesize ideas drawn from a variety of authors, contexts, and genres while incorporating some observations of my own on the subject.

I have often had occasion to transfer or apply ideas originally expressed in contexts very different from this one to a discussion of human life and death. It has been my observation that the "wisdom" we seek concerning ultimate questions of life and death is found in this rather nebulous body of literature more readily than in either the religious texts of old or in more contemporary books on the subject. Novelists in particular often attain a more profound understanding of human existence than authors of other genres, including most philosophers. (The main exception to this I would identify as the late nineteenth century German philosopher Friedrich Nietzsche, whose understanding of the human spirit and the human condition as a totality remains, in my view, unrivaled to this day. Were we familiar with more of his observations, and with the observations of several of those whom he inspired, major portions of this book would have been unnecessary.

CHAPTER 1
THE ENCOUNTER WITH DEATH

1

Shock and escape. The awareness of death confronts the mind as
nothing else. Be it the death of a loved one or one's own impending
end, the sense of death no longer as an abstract possibility but as an
immediate certainty commands attention in a manner wholly unlike
any other experience. In an instant the preoccupations of everyday
life recede from view and anxiety gives way to numbness and disorientation, leaving our sense of self and of reality in temporary sus-
pension; a single obstinate fact stands before us.

As long as death remains a topic of abstract discussion, we are
all philosophers. We speak with great detachment of death as an
inevitability and a certainty, we muse over its mystery and our anticipation of a life beyond this life. Few topics are more subject to
cliché, known to us all and quotable as the occasion demands. Yet
there is a sense in which death remains radically unexpected, no
matter what the abstract certainties or the prognosis of the physi-

cian. Death leaves us, as Sigmund Freud observed, "shaken by the unexpected,"[1] as if somewhere in the inner recesses of our being we did not altogether believe in the reality of death — most especially our own.

That death happens, we understand perfectly. It is even inevitable and inescapable. For human beings in the abstract, it is a daily occurrence and quite as it ought to be; for acquaintances, it is a sobering inevitability, while for loved ones it is altogether unexpected, and for oneself it is unthinkable. This universal human phenomenon is described by Leo Tolstoy in *The Death of Ivan Ilych*: "The syllogism he had leant from Kiesewetter's Logic: 'Caius is a man, men are mortal, therefore Caius is mortal,' had always seemed to him correct as applied to Caius, but certainly not as applied to himself. That Caius — man in the abstract — was mortal, was perfectly correct, but he was not Caius, not an abstract man, but a creature quite, quite separate from all others."[2]

Coexisting uneasily within each of us are dark realizations, impossible to deny, and comforting reassurances that we shall not be without. If a note of falsity characterizes many, perhaps most, familiar attitudes toward death, it is no doubt on account of the instinct of avoidance which here reaches a fever pitch. Among the strategies of avoidance devised by human beings, the code of silence is among the most common. Discussion of this most indelicate subject continues to invite general indignation and horror, as if declaring death a topic unfit for discussion would somehow lessen its severity or perhaps abolish it altogether. Like sex in Victorian England, death must be spoken of — if at all — in hushed tones, not in the presence of children, only in specific contexts, and by appropriate personages.

A second strategy, not unlike the first, often accompanies the code of silence. This is, as Freud also observed, "to downgrade death from a necessity to a fortuitous happening,"[3] perhaps even to an unnatural occurrence. One of the most frequently asked questions in the event of the death of someone close to us is, "Why her?" — as if death were a mere happenstance from which a kinder fate might have spared her.

We grasp at a surface level of consciousness that death happens, but why must it happen precisely to her, why now, and more to the point, why to me? The philosopher in each of us replies sternly, "Why not her? Her it shall be — and everyone else besides." Yet another voice chimes in, with private indignation, that we too shall cease to exist as the person we now are, and perhaps cease to exist in any form. The terror and unnaturalness of it all compels us to seek reassurance that all is not lost, and that, in any event, it is not as bad as it seems. The quest for reassurance is often one in which intellectual honesty, or even the well-being of the dying, are quickly sacrificed. The reticence and deception about death which Tolstoy described as the harshest cruelty inflicted on the dying by relatives and care givers involves the refusal to look death in the face by denying its reality, minimizing its significance, or diverting attention. It is a deception supported by medical institutions, the funeral industry, and the various funereal accouterments. Everything from the life-like appearance of the corpse to the names of cemeteries and funeral homes gives the appearance of death as an unreality, a condition closely related to sleep, or perhaps a temporary illness.

2

Escape through religion. When silence, distraction, and deception fail us as means of coping with death — as at the physician's prognosis or the sight of the corpse they so often do — one final appeal is traditionally made. This is the appeal to religion, with all its solemnity, pageantry, and institutional authority. The accounts it provides of a life to come superior to this vale of tears served for centuries as an effective palliative against death, and for a decreasing number it continues to do so. That each of the great religions offered psychologically satisfying promises of rebirth or salvation is undoubtedly among the reasons they gained victory over their ancient competitors and survived through the centuries. In offering victory over death in the form of an afterlife or superior rebirth, life itself came to be viewed as a preparation for death, and death in a sense as the goal of life.

In the West, for example, Christianity held out the promise of an unearthly paradise where the victory over death would be complete. It offered consolation against the fear of death and for the sufferings of this life. It devised stories of redemption and rituals whose ostensible aim was to facilitate acceptance of physical death, but whose psychological function was to solemnize and spiritualize the evasion of death. Like a child seeking protection from a harsh environment, there is a part of human nature that has always sought solace against death from a parental surrogate, a role that religious institutions have long served. The reassurance of an afterlife promises to deliver us from all anxiety — to lie — while in so doing depriving us of the means that enable us to come to terms both with death and with life.

In confronting one's own death or mourning another, we may hope for a life beyond this life and to see the loved one again, yet we can know with certainty no such thing. We encounter the limits of human knowledge often when it is least convenient psychologically, and it is plain deception to claim certainty over what does not admit of it. The deception that religion fosters regarding death is not innocent. It obliges us to surrender our autonomy and intellectual honesty when our task is precisely to set these capacities to work in the search for meaningful and peaceful resolution. It invites us to conceive of death as an event with a fixed meaning to which we must passively resign ourselves rather than an experience for which we must create a meaning. We come to terms with death not in taking palliatives or heeding authoritative exhortations of acceptance, but in understanding what makes mature acceptance possible and undertaking to bring this about.

We have traditionally coped with death by refusing to contemplate it and by lying, hoping that such measures would bring comfort to the dying and to the bereaved. The prospect of personal annihilation is one we would adopt virtually any means to defeat, yet the measures we have taken are suited only to a species not yet come of age intellectually and spiritually. The refusal to look death in the face is not only ineffective as a strategy for coping with the end of life, but is symptomatic of the refusal to look upon life itself. We would avoid death at any price, yet is it really life that we seek or, on the contrary, is it the security that arrests life?

Is there not some truth in Fyodor Dostoyevsky's assertion that "we have all lost touch with life" in the quest for security, even tutelage? (Dostoyevsky expressed these provocative but accurate words through the character of the underground man in *Notes From Under-*

ground: "In fact, we have lost touch so badly that we often feel a kind of loathing for genuine 'living life,' and hence cannot endure being reminded of it. We've reached a point where we virtually regard 'living life' as hard labor, almost servitude, and we all agree in private that it's much better 'according to books.' And why do we sometimes fidget, why do we fuss, what are we asking for? We ourselves don't know, for, after all, it will be worse for us if our silly whims are granted. Just try, just give us, for example, more independence; untie the hands of any one of us, broaden our scope of action, relax the tutelage over us, and we. . . . [w]hy, I assure you, we shall immediately beg to be placed under tutelage again."[4])

Further, has this evasion not become the greatest obstacle to accepting and coming to terms with death? The shock and unexpectedness of death are not unrelated to the escapism I have described, but are direct consequences of the refusal to contemplate in an intellectually honest manner the phenomena of human death and life.

3

Death as wake-up call. So much of human life is lived in a mist that we require periodic reminding of what is ultimate in human existence. Like drivers on a long stretch of road, we are intent on the tenth of a mile immediately before us, forgetting both where we are heading and from where we have come, the condition of our vehicle, and the rules of the road. There is nothing unusual or especially objectionable in this. It is a habit we fall into with the greatest of ease, yet coming out of it is a different matter entirely. As if aware of this, life itself occasionally brings us back, sometimes with a vengeance, to what the ways of the world invite us to forget.

The fact that we are physical organisms whose existence is contingent, unstable, and of limited duration is for many a morbid reflection we are foolish to dwell upon. Yet in casting this reflection aside and limiting attention to the preoccupations of everyday life, what results is not only a forgetfulness of death — something perhaps not unfortunate in itself — but a forgetfulness of life.

The awareness of death serves better than any other thought to invite, sometimes to force, a refocusing on what is of ultimate importance. In confronting one's own mortality, or experiencing the death of someone close, we are brought back to ourselves in the most radical way possible. Our perspective cannot but return to matters we had put out of mind or postponed for a later date, such matters as the ultimate significance of our lives and the connection between this and our everyday projects. The degree to which we overlook such matters is the degree that the confrontation with death returns us with a jolt from the narrowness of daily life to the broader perspective required for understanding matters of life and death.

It is in understanding the singular power of death to awaken us to life that the value of these reflections may be seen. They serve at once the philosophical purpose of rendering explicit an elementary phenomenon of human existence as well as the urgently practical problem of how issues of death and dying may be approached in a way that makes possible peaceful acceptance and meaningful resolution without sacrificing intellectual honesty. The hypothesis that guides this study is that contemplating death affords a perspective for understanding life and the life process of which death is a part. Death loses its appearance as a brute fact or morbid occurrence when it is reinterpreted in the larger context of the processes of life in which we are all participants, as well as an occasion to exercise our freedom.

4

The value of anxiety. Existential philosophy often distinguishes anxiety from fear. While the latter invariably possesses a definite object — the dreaded event, the approaching disaster — anxiety is a deeper apprehension with respect to human existence itself and to one's possible nonexistence. The experience of anxiety marks an interruption in the concerns of everyday life and brings into view the possibility of nothingness and, closely related to this, that of personal mortality. Unlike objects of fear, which we may struggle against and ultimately defeat, no final victory over anxiety is within our grasp.

While medicine and psychology are often inclined to regard anxiety as symptomatic by nature of mental disturbance, hence something that we may hope to eliminate through appropriate therapy, anxiety is more properly regarded as belonging to the very nature of human existence. It is an experience that may be ignored or repressed, but it cannot be "cured" for the reason that anxiety is not in itself pathological.

Moreover, anxiety is an experience that is not without value for those who look upon it as an occasion to see beyond the narrowness and distraction of ordinary life to the deeper conditions that underlie it. The encounter with death is an education, awakening us from the habitual inattention to life that alienates us from ourselves and from the deeper meaning that our lives hold. It is an encounter that not only recommits us to life, but provides an occasion to reexamine our habitual ways of living and acting.

Above all, the experience of anxiety compels us to exercise our freedom in a manner well described by philosopher Martin Heidegger.[5] This is a freedom that may be exercised in the direction of greater authenticity, a way of being in which the individual chooses, and thereby takes responsibility for, himself or herself and the fundamental direction of his or her life. Conscious acts of choice are the means by which the various elements of a life become authentically one's own. Alternatively, the encounter with anxiety and death can lead toward an inauthentic flight from oneself, a flight into conformity with convention or authority. In either case, the experience of death leaves one altered, aware of one's capacity for freedom and the obligation to exercise it in one direction or the other. It eliminates, if temporarily, all thoughtlessness and triviality, revealing to each of us the human condition as it really is and the extent of our freedom within it.

5

The turn within. The confrontation with death is unique in its capacity to alter in the most radical manner the perspective, and with it the very being, of the individual. It is remarkable not only for the distractions and trivialities that it places out of view, but for that which it places fully before our view. It calls the individual away from small matters of everyday concern and toward his own inner depths.

Psychologists often describe the unsociability and diminishing interests of mourners and dying persons as symptomatic of depression or shock, which often accompany the diagnosis of terminal illness and the experience of mourning. The withdrawal, unresponsiveness, and unconcern with objects of prior interest have been compared with the psychological aftereffects of disasters of various kinds, the premise often being that such a condition, like anxiety, is invariably pathological. What these accounts often overlook is that the mourner's, or the dying person's, condition is not only a turning away, but a turning toward — and, more specifically, a turning within.

The imperative to turn within to the inner regions of the self most likely is universally characteristic of human existence. It is an imperative heeded not only by artists and poets, but by persons generally and in a great variety of ways. All inspiration, private reflection, and creativity have their source here, in a realm of inwardness and unsociability. The artist, as convention has it, labors in the isolation of a studio, the craftsman toils in the privacy of a shop, the scientist devises inventions and concoctions in a laboratory, while the prophet finds enlightenment on the loneliest mountaintop. These are clichés, to be sure, and clichés that conceal much about the nature of human thought and creativity. Yet what they reveal at a deeper level of analysis is perhaps more notable still. What such notions evidence is an understanding of inwardness as a condition of our being fully human and of engaging the world in an efficacious way. One turns within not as an escapist flight from reality, but precisely as a condition of authentic engagement with reality.

While not alone in experiencing this inward imperative, the dying are in the unique and unwelcome condition of having no recourse to comfortable evasions, being virtually compelled to look death in the face. The encounter that had been postponed for a later date can no longer be evaded and, like what Freud termed "the return of the repressed," one is confronted with the most unsettling realizations, with redoubled force.

In light of the escapism toward death which I have described, it is especially unsurprising that persons diagnosed with terminal illness and mourners often feel so thoroughly undermined in the encounter with death, and depressive pathology can be the result. Yet the withdrawal and seeming indifference of such persons, which appear to the onlooker to signal the onset of depression, may instead, or simultaneously, indicate something else entirely. This is a turning into the deeper and interior regions of the self, an encounter with oneself, one's personal past, and the ultimate significance of one's life. For some, this turning within is virtually without precedent in their lives, while for others it is of unprecedented intensity and urgency. Its mortal adversaries are the evasion and pretense of ordinary life which effectively alienate the self from its interior depths, the dimension of the personality that finally demands its due.

6

Death as the ground of individuality. At the same time that this inward imperative calls us back from the realm of practical necessity and "worldliness" to the inner recesses of the self, we are brought face to face both with our mortality and with our individuality. Death provides the ground or basis of our individuality in the sense that we die invariably as individuals, departing the world as we entered it. Even in the romantic scene of two lovers dying in each other's arms, there is a deeper sense in which one's death is absolutely one's own, an experience that cannot be shared. Our death belongs to us in the way that our birth does — hopefully our lives as well — as unique persons, unsubstitutable, and in a condition from which no one can deliver us.

A familiar saying has it that no one can die our death for us, that we each face the prospect of dying not as social beings, but alone. The encounter with death is profoundly isolating, not only for those who are overcome by despair and "dead to the world," but for us all. It is an encounter that, in the traditional view, is a morbid indulgence, perhaps even a threat to the integrity of the personality. We look upon those overcome by grief as having fallen into an abyss away from which we must run, not walk. And yet, if it is an experience that is authentically faced, the confrontation with death can alter radically our understanding of ourselves and the world, enhancing the sense of individuality and the taste for life which our day-to-day existence leads us to overlook. Those who work with the terminally ill often speak of a pronounced authenticity and sincerity frequently exhibited by the dying, as if they recognize that the time for evasion and forgetfulness of life is now past.

Both dying persons and those who mourn them face the task of standing back from the affairs of everyday life and heeding the instinct to recall ourselves as individuals. This is an instinct that counsels not despair or withdrawal from life, but temporary retreat in order the better to participate in life. The affirmation of personal separateness, likewise, is not the gloomy assertion that "we are all alone in the world," but is instead a precondition of all meaningful and honest sociability.

7

The question of meaning. Between religious conceptions of death or the afterlife as the ultimate goal and meaning of human existence, and secular views in which life's highest purpose can never be separated from the process of living itself, there is little room for compromise. The former, notably the Christian, view tends to speak of this earthly existence as if it were a dress rehearsal of sorts for a life to come — one, it must be said, for which the evidence is meager. It warns against secular worldviews which, as it claims, deprive human life of lasting significance and hope, by locating us in a universe indifferent to human concerns. The secular reply has it that while the universe itself does appear remarkably unmoved by human trials and tribulations, this is no cause for despair since it is not from "the point of view of the universe" that human life gains significance, but from the point of view of life itself, and specifically our own. The meaning that our lives hold for us is not writ large or carved into the very fabric of the universe, but is an interpretation fashioned by each of us in the course of living.

It is an ancient prejudice that the significance of human life must transcend life itself, that it is held aloft in the heavens, unchanged for all time — or else it is limited to the vulgar pleasures, or absent altogether. The same view has it that there is and can be but one meaning of human existence, a meaning that is universal, timeless, and absolute. That we must choose between these two extremes has long been assumed by so many that it often seems as if we are compelled by the very nature of things to affirm either a world without meaning — the one described by modern science — or a world inhabited and ruled by the gods, either a life without significance or one in which the question of significance is fixed for all time.

The dimension of human nature that insists on all matters of first importance being absolute once and for all, from the nature of justice and truth to the ultimate significance of life itself, has often in history spoken with the loudest voice, if not the subtlest or most honest one. A more honest questioning into the notion of a "meaningful life," or a meaningful death, is not unlike the kind of inquiry we undertake in the course of everyday life into the meaning of a sentence, an action, or a text. In no case do we find a meaning that is altogether fixed, but one that calls for interpretation. It is a meaning that is "for us," in the sense that it emerges from the questions we put to it and it fits into a framework of concerns and understandings that we carry with us. The meaning of a work of literature emerges in the reading of it; it is neither fixed nor eternal, nor does it depend on the pronouncement of authority. The significance of an action, gesture, or historical event likewise calls for interpretation and takes shape in the interchange between interpreter and interpreted object. Why life as a whole should be different in this respect from the elements that comprise it defies explanation.

8

Death and perspective. It is a dangerous proposition to conceive of the purpose of human existence as anything beyond that existence itself, whether it be a life to come or a promised land of religion. Yet while death is in no sense the meaning or purpose of life, it does offer a perspective from which that meaning may be appropriately understood. The encounter with death provides an opportunity, albeit an unwelcome one, to understand the significance of a life that is now at an end. This is owing not only to our habitual refusal to contemplate such matters, but to the nature of human understanding itself.

We understand a work of literature in reading through to its end and looking back from the perspective it provides on the events that came before. The working understanding that had sustained us through previous chapters is now replaced with one fully informed by the course of the narrative and by the consequences of prior events. In arriving at the end, we comprehend the work as a whole, seeing individual events not as isolated occurrences, but in light of other events, particularly their long-term consequences. It is characteristic of human understanding to operate in reverse, or after the fact. Only thus is it possible for us to gain the perspective necessary for perceiving an object or event in its entirety rather than as an ongoing process awaiting conclusion.

This principle applies no less to human lives than to works of literature. Upon death, an individual's life becomes in a sense a *fait accompli*, one that may be conceived as a whole with an identifiable beginning, middle, and end. In reaching its end, a life is experienced no longer as an anticipation of possibilities, but as an actuality. Ideally, it is an actuality in the sense not only of a brute fact, but of realized potentiality, although as we well know this is far from always the case.

The death of an individual provides an occasion for reflection in two senses. It makes it possible for us to gain a more complete, retrospective understanding of the life that is now at an end while also, in a sense, compelling us to do so. Unless their life and death be an object of indifference to us, it becomes imperative to contemplate the life that is now past and to come to terms with its passing. This "coming to terms" is again bound up with a context of meaning in which an element of closure can be gained. To come to terms with a person's death is inseparable from coming to terms with their life, the significance of both being intimately related.[6]

It is in answering the "what for?" questions — what is this death for? what was this life for? — that meaning is imposed on an event that in itself contains no meaning. What positive value did that life bring about? What potential did it realize? What influence did it have? What lessons does it teach? These are the questions that are posed to us in our efforts to find closure and come to terms with death, be it one's own or another's. Indeed, what is a "meaningful death" but closure to a meaningful life?

9

Grief work. Mature acceptance of death is so far from being a merely passive resignation to the inevitable that psychologists now speak of "grief work," a phrase that correctly suggests that grieving needs to be taken on as a task. Yet what sort of task is this? Is it not somewhat indelicate to suggest that persons confronting their mortality or bereaved by loss must take up a project which, on the face of it, appears to be of some difficulty? Traditional views, as we have seen, run so far in the opposite direction that in the name of compassion or decency the grieving are spared every effort possible, including especially any direct encounter or preoccupation with death.

Yet, as psychologists now recognize, avoidance strategies of all kinds, whether it be of death or a traumatic experience of another sort, invariably fail in their purpose.

Grieving is a process that must be "worked through," to use Freud's term, or digested through conversation, understanding, and the expression of emotion. Simple repression of grief is not only counterproductive psychologically, but contrary to the desire (usually spontaneous, to the dying and the bereaved) to discuss and express fully the emotions associated with grieving. It is now a commonplace that anesthetizing unwelcome emotion merely drives it underground, delaying for a time its full expression, only for it to return with redoubled force at a later date or in alternate form. The prudery many feel toward death often creates a barrier between the dying or bereaved and those around them, where the former wish to confront directly the experience they are undergoing while the latter seek flight.

Human experience in general requires something very much akin, psychologically and cognitively, to digestion, from the most ordinary events of everyday life to the momentous experiences of coping with loss and confronting our mortality. It requires a capacity to confront directly and honestly the experiences that shape our lives and, in the case we are considering, a willingness to cut through the barriers that tradition erects in order to penetrate to a deeper level of emotional awareness. The dying and grieving processes both lead us into the very depths of our being, and while this is a territory (an "internal foreign territory," as Freud would say) in which we are not altogether at home, working through these processes compels us to descend to the psychological level at which grief has its source.

The experiences most frequently identified by psychologists as characteristic of the dying process include denial and isolation, anger, bargaining with a higher power, depression, acceptance, and hope. These experiences, which are not altogether different from the emotions experienced by the grieving, are claimed by psychologist Elisabeth Kubler-Ross to constitute distinct and universal "stages" passed through in the course of dying and in the order here listed.[7] Since Kubler-Ross's investigations, other observers have noted similarities in the emotional responses of the terminally ill while rejecting that author's assertion that these are discrete stages passed through in a definite and predictable order. Psychologist Edwin Shneidman, for instance, describes more subtly ". . . a hive of affect, in which there is a constant coming and going. The emotional stages seem to include a constant interplay between disbelief and hope and, against these as background, a waxing and waning of anguish, terror, acquiescence and surrender, rage and envy, disinterest and ennui, pretense, taunting and daring and even yearning for death — all these in the context of bewilderment and pain."[8]

There is very little in human experience that can be measured and predicted with mathematical exactitude, and it is unlikely in the extreme that something as momentous and subterranean as the grieving and dying processes should conform to so simple a model as that described by Kubler-Ross, or to any model. Social scientists do love their theoretical models, statistical regularities, and abstract techniques, sometimes at the expense of oversimplifying and glossing over the phenomena as they present themselves to our unscientific understanding. Yet one observation that does seem to represent not only a statistical regularity but a genuine necessity is that persons coping with death must experience directly and express fully the conflicting emotions arising from one's own or another's death.

10

Unfinished business. Additional to what I have stated above regarding the inward or intrapersonal matter of working through the levels of emotion experienced in any authentic encounter with death is the task of leaving no "unfinished business" in our personal relationships. This imperative has its source not in any externally imposed morality, but in an inward need to "get one's affairs in order" or to eliminate "loose ends." Each of these expressions bespeaks a deeper imperative within the self to integrate in one fashion or other the relationships and projects of everyday life into an arrangement free of contradiction, a task expressed in the notion of integrity. This imperative or task belongs to each of us in the general course of living and is by no means limited to those presently confronting the reality of death. Here again, however, is a task that our daily preoccupations often lead us to ignore or postpone, until the encounter with death compels us to make order of our disordered existence.

A common undertaking of dying persons, for instance, is to renew old relationships and either seek or grant forgiveness to those from whom we are estranged. Whether the frequency of such eleventh hour transformations is more owing to a fortunate peculiarity of the dying or to the shortcomings and evasions of the living is a riddle I do not propose to solve. What we do know is that persons facing death most often confront this other task with a determination and honesty unusual among the rest of us. The elimination of matters incomplete, discordant, or unresolved, the remedying of disruptions in personal relationships, and so on, are tasks peculiar to no subset of humanity, yet the instinct to undertake them is especially acute to persons confronting their mortality.

II

The choice of life or death. Psychologists tell us that to grieve properly we must emote completely rather than repress the affects connected with loss. As creatures of passion, we digest experiences of profound significance by expressing freely the emotions that those

experiences evoke. This observation has become something of a commonplace in recent years among psychologists and the general public
alike.

What is not commonplace are a couple of related observations
on the subject of grief work. First, since the human being is not
only, as psychologists tell us, a creature of passion but, as philosophers tell us, a rational being, we work through the grieving process
by understanding — not lying about — the significance of death,
the extent of our loss, and the meaning that the life which is now at
an end holds for us. This also is grief work, and it is a concentrated
form of the task of living itself.

Second, as free agents it is a life task of each of us to choose
with conscious will and purpose both a particular way of living and
indeed whether to live at all. It is the latter question that the process of grieving often brings into especially sharp focus, despite the
taboos and superstitions that surround the issue of suicide. Our personal existence is so deeply linked with the lives of emotionally significant persons that in the event of their loss — particularly that of
a life partner of many years — the idea of suicide may be welcomed
as a consolation or, in the unfathomable logic of the unconscious, as
an opportunity for reunion. As Nietzsche remarked, "the thought of
suicide is a powerful comfort: it helps one through many a dreadful
night."[9]

The currently orthodox view of suicide as almost invariably a
product of mental illness, hence not an act that may be chosen
freely, overlooks almost completely that the will to live is itself a
contingency, and not only among the mentally ill. There are conditions in life in which our very existence is experienced as a burden,
whether owing to the death of someone close, grievous illness, inhu-

man treatment, or other personal misfortune. Not one of us is in a position to judge for others what level of suffering they ought to bear. Nor is it our place to burden such persons further with purported moral obligations to continue an existence disagreeable to them for the sake of others, or with ancient superstitions that our lives do not belong to us but to an invisible power.

The choice of life or death in the face of suffering is less a "moral issue" in the usual sense of the term than an existential decision. I shall return to this point in a later chapter, but for now I would suggest that the question of the moral permissibility of suicide is secondary to the existential issue of the will to live in the face of suffering. This is a choice that belongs to each of us as free agents, yet the decision to confront it directly, rather than to let it go without saying or to shirk the issue as taboo, is crucial both to the process of grieving and to the more basic task of being human. Psychologist Rollo May has noted a few of the beneficial implications that follow upon the explicit choice of life or death, beginning with "a heightened awareness of life, a heightened sense of possibility." Beyond this, May observes: "When one has consciously chosen to live, two other things happen. First, his responsibility for himself takes on a new meaning. He accepts responsibility for his own life not as something with which he has been saddled, a burden forced upon him: but as a something he has chosen, himself. For this person, himself, now exists as a result of a decision he himself has made. . . . The other thing which happens is that discipline from the outside is changed into *self-discipline*. He accepts discipline not because it is commanded — for who can command someone who has been free to take his own life? — but because he has chosen with greater freedom what he wants to do with his own life, and discipline is necessary for the sake of the values he wishes to achieve."[10] How often we hear it said, particularly by the very young, that we did not choose to be born — as if to demonstrate the unfreedom of one's condition, while it is closer to the truth to suppose that one chooses continu-ally both whether to continue one's life and what ends will guide it.

The single most momentous decision in human life is the choice of life or death in the face of suffering, and it is not a question that admits of a uniform answer. It requires an existential choice, with all the consequences that follow upon it — either an end to this life or a renewed commitment to a life that is freely chosen. This is a choice that, while belonging to each of us, becomes especially pressing within the grieving process. It is, as Schneidman accurately observes, a choice that most often is not made explicitly, but "subintentionally." Shneidman speaks of "subintentioned death" as ". . . one in which the person plays some partial, covert, subliminal or unconscious role in hastening his own demise. The evidence for such a role might be found in a variety of behavior patterns: poor judgment, imprudence, excessive risk-taking, neglect of self, disre-gard of a life-extending medical regimen, abuse of alcohol, misuse of drugs — all ways in which an individual can advance the date of his death."[11]

The phenomenon of subintentioned suicide, in which the indi-vidual plays an unwitting but participative role in facilitating death, is, he suggests, far more common than is usually supposed. While extremely difficult to identify, it likely includes a large percentage of deaths deemed "accidental," particularly among those who have re-cently suffered a grievous loss. It is a familiar fact, for example, that many widows and widowers die within a relatively short time of their life partner. It is at such a time that the contingency of the will to live becomes most visible, although a contingency it has always been.

12

The Death of Ivan Ilych. There are few, and perhaps no, observers of the human situation more astute than Leo Tolstoy, as the classic story to which I have referred previously gives ample evidence. *The Death of Ivan Ilych* recounts the final days of a high-ranking public official whose life had been spent in the pursuit of social position and the more "refined" pleasures that typically accompany it. His belief in the dignity of his office and general manner of living never came into question for Ilych until the realization of his impending death forced him into a re-examination of his life. This re-examination well illustrates several of the hypotheses touched on above, from the shock and unreality of death to the turn within, the search for meaning, and the honest realization of what has been.

Ilych's self-examination reveals what was previously unthinkable: that his entire existence has been one of falsity, role-playing, and mean-spiritedness. Beneath the niceties of propriety and duty lay a disconnection from the vital process of living. Not since childhood had Ilych wholly participated in life, nor had the colleagues and relatives whom he now despises as mirror reflections of himself. The encounter with death reveals for the first time the truth of his life, with unbearable suffering as the consequence. Here tradition would dictate that one avoid all such self-examination if it dampened one's mood, particularly if this became visible to others who might be forced by the sight of human suffering into a similar reflection. Heeding tradition, Ilych's wife and colleagues are scornfully turned away by a man who has no one to speak to about this, the final and most momentous occurrence of his life, except for a sympathetic servant who has himself accepted gracefully his own fini-tude. The self-deception Ilych now sees both in his own life and in the lives of all those around him concerns not only the estrangement from death but — inseparable from this — an estrangement from life.

What Ilych perceives clearly throughout the course of the nar-rative is the imperative to understand honestly what his life has been for. It is a subject that engrosses him completely until the painful realization that everything in his life has been false, and that this realization would die with him. Yet it is the recognition of what his life has been, and what it ought to have been, that brings a de-gree of redemption for Ilych, who from the moment of his realiza-tion refuses the pretense by which he had lived. In accepting this most painful realization, death loses its victory over Ilych, even as he succumbs to it.

13

Death as educator. For Ivan Ilych, the confrontation with death was the supreme educator, forcing him into the most honest intro-spection of his life and examination of others' lives as well. His life now a *fait accompli*, he is able to identify the moral of his own life story, something possible as well for witnesses of that life. Indeed, it is here that we find one of the most imperative tasks of grieving: learning the lessons that a life now at an end teaches. This is done either in the form of consciously adopting aspects of the deceased's personality or way of life, or the opposite: making a conscious choice not to follow the example.

If the latter seems harsh, consider the familiar occurrence of a person whose life is cut short owing to addiction, inordinate risk-taking, or an unwise lifestyle choice. We do our tactful best in such circumstances to avoid overt statements of blame, yet in our private moments there is nothing untoward in identifying cause and effect, and in choosing to avoid the cause. The ability to learn from others' mistakes no less than one's own is among the more valuable capacities one could acquire, if not one of the more common.

More frequently, grieving involves an education of a more positive kind. This begins with a recognition of what the life of the deceased contributed or "meant," followed by the survivors' decision to take upon themselves some trait or interest of the deceased.

Individual character is invariably an incorporation of the personalities to which we are exposed, particularly in childhood. In no case does the self take shape in a social and cultural vacuum, but through a creative and largely unconscious appropriation of character traits, attitudes, and ways of living belonging to persons in one's environment. The result is a self of no small complexity, likely far more complex than we are accustomed to supposing. Psychologist Henry Murray makes this point in rather dramatic terms. "A personality is a full congress of orators and pressure-groups, of children, demagogues, communists, isolationists, war-mongers, mugwumps, grafters, log-rollers, lobbyists, Caesars and Christs, Machiavellis and Judases, Tories and Promethean revolutionists."[12] The complexity of the human personality is compounded further by the freedom of individual to modify their own character with conscious will and purpose, identifying traits that they do not presently possess (or possess in a minor degree) and taking them upon themselves.   While the freedom to accomplish this is not without limits, it is a mistake to view character as fixed or beyond our capacity to modify. Refashioning character, from what we merely are to what we aspire to be, is a task undertaken by each of us in the course of our lives, even if much of this task is carried out unconsciously or semi-consciously.

Incorporating traits from persons in our environment is something at which children are expert. Much of a child's character is a synthesis of traits learned from parents, siblings, and other figures in his or her life. In reaching maturity, this synthesis becomes potentially one of increasing complexity, creativity, and freedom. The observation of "role models," acquaintances, or literary figures combined with a degree of reflection and an act of will makes possible a limited refashioning of the self. The death of someone close is an occasion to carry this into practice, as we reflect upon the more admirable qualities of the deceased and the lessons that their life imparts. This "learning" is not merely an intellectual but, for lack of a better expression, a "spiritual" exercise which reaches potentially into the innermost dimensions of our character.

Incorporating traits of the deceased into oneself goes beyond simple acts of self-improvement to restoring the integrity of personality which that death may have threatened. The death of a parent, for example, who from childhood has been not only a profound influence on one's character but in a sense an extension or dimension of that character, can be profoundly destabilizing. The pain of loss is coupled with what survivors commonly describe as the death of "a part of themselves," an expression that is almost literally true as a description of what has happened to them. In such a case, personality is restored by reviving the other within, cultivating the dimension of character that the deceased represents to us. The simple act of remembering the deceased, or taking up one of their characteristic habits or interests, also promotes this end.

14

Death as an action. Death, we often hear it said, is among the most inescapable certainties of human existence. It is an altogether given fact — one that may be postponed or ignored, but not eluded. In this respect it would seem to defy action, yet it is in action and in the exercise of our freedom that we appear most fully human. The "human spirit," they say, challenges inevitabilities and defies odds, yet here we encounter an adversary against which struggle or any effective action at all appears futile. How, then, does one meet death as a human being, that is, not only as a living organism, but as an agent possessed of freedom? In encountering death, do we abandon the very capacities that sustained us in life, or do we put them to work the more urgently still?

Death is not, as we are accustomed to thinking, merely an event that befalls us, but is in an important respect an action and task which the dying person takes up. One's death, like one's life, is something that one must make one's own — through an act of will, or through a series of these. Except for cases of sudden and unexpected death, the dying person becomes a participant in a process comprising a series of tasks as I have described above. They must "get their affairs in order" and leave no "unfinished business." They face imperatives of reflection, introspection, and withdrawal from all matters of unimportance. Their death becomes human in being invested with meaning, and it becomes their own in having imposed on it a meaning, a manner, and in some cases a timing of their choosing. A meaningful death, as Nietzsche recognized, has an air of consummation to it; it is the consummation of a meaningful life, one "which shall be a spur and a promise to the living."[13]

A death that marks not only the end but the consummation of a life is one in which there is a degree of continuity between the person known to us in life and the person facing death. Socrates, confronting his own imminent death, remained a philosopher to the end, electing to spend his final moments in philosophical conversation rather than plotting escape from execution. In dying as he had lived, and for the principles by which he had lived, Socrates had his death take on an eminently human, even heroic, quality, and mainly for this reason it remains among the most notable deaths of human history.

The death that is an action and a consummation, rather than merely an event that happens to us, is in part subject to the will of the dying person. That one must die is a given fact about which one can do nothing, but in many cases how one dies, or even when one dies, are matters that do permit of some freedom. To face death with relatively little unresolved, with an understanding of the ends one's life has served, is to die as one has lived, and in a sense is akin to having completed a task.

In certain instances, the timing of one's death is also an issue of some considerable freedom. As the movement in favor of the "living will," the right to die, and preemptive suicide gives evidence, the issue of the freedom to choose the timing and manner of one's own death is becoming increasingly pressing. As growing numbers demand alternatives to the institutionalization of death which has become a commonplace of modern life, the idea is beginning to dawn that certain forms of suicide — by the terminally ill or those confronting the knowledge of impending and irreversible decline — may be less an act of despair or resignation than one of self-definition and autonomy. (I shall return to this issue in Chapter 3.)

15

Rebellion and necessity. From the beginnings of human history, we have realized that the attitude of rebellion is in many ways funda-mental to what it means to be human. History is replete with rebels both mythical and real, from Adam, Prometheus, and Socrates to Voltaire, Jean-Jacques Rousseau, and Thomas Jefferson. To such de-fiers we owe not only much of our freedom, but a fundamental un-derstanding of the human condition. Through their efforts we have come to conceive the situation of human beings as crucially involv-ing the overcoming of servility, ignorance, suffering, and also neces-sity — particularly natural necessity. Is it not, then, in a sense, the human spirit itself that has us deny the reality of death, the natural necessity *par excellence*, or perhaps to look beyond it to a life beyond this life?

What I have described above as the traditional evasion of death resembles less an authentic gesture of rebellion than one of dishonesty and escape. While it is wholly understandable that death should make cowards of almost all of us (the main exceptions, I suspect, being those who either contemplate death the least or lie about it the most), the most difficult task in any authentic encoun-ter with death is the apparently simple act of seeing it for what it is. Acknowledging fully the reality of death — one's own or an-other's — without lying is a demanding but inescapable task, one made still more difficult by the falsity that typically surrounds death. This is a falsity and intellectual dishonesty that, in the story of Ivan Ilych, "did more than anything else to poison his last days."[14] Facing the truth in the midst of sorrow is as difficult as it is rare. It is, moreover, an act that resembles rebellion more than submission to necessity. This is a rebellion that refuses all comforting reassurance and false consolation, the rebellion that says yes to life while knowing fully that it too will end.

"Insight into necessity," philosopher Herbert Marcuse writes, "is the first step toward the dissolution of necessity."[15] The acceptance of facts, no matter how sobering, makes it possible to live authentically as a human being, which means in part living in the face of death. It means reconciling ourselves with the human condition, with our finitude, and with that which stands against us, even as we prepare to stand against it. It means exercising the capacities and attitudes in the face of death that we exercise in the course of our lives, hence encountering death as we encounter life. Rebellion defies death not by pretending or wishing it were not so, but by refusing to relinquish the capacities and dispositions, including honesty and freedom, that sustained us in life.

So pervasive is the dishonesty about death, from the different forms of escapism described above to the glowing tributes to the deceased heard in conventional eulogies, that it seems the value we place on truthfulness and intellectual honesty in the course of our lives all but disappears in the face of death. While the truth does not always set us free, shrinking from it almost never does so. The recognition of what we cannot change, as well as what we cannot know, is the beginning both of intellectual wisdom and of psychological maturity. Recognition in the face of suffering provides their surest measure.

16

Foreshadowings of death. While the encounter with death is undeniably unique, it is an experience that is not without foreshadowings at other times in our lives. Human experience is invariably temporal; it takes place in the present but is also experienced as arising from a personal past, anticipating a future. So inseparable is human experience from the movement of time that the individual self (as I have argued elsewhere[16]) may be likened to a story unfolding through time with a beginning, a middle, and an end. It is a narrative in which the "I" is always the principal character acting within a context of major and minor characters, plots and subplots, and a variety of themes and episodes arranged in complex order while displaying a semblance of direction. If one's birth marks the beginning of the story that one is, then death clearly represents the end.

Yet it is characteristic of a well-told narrative to be divided not only into particular episodes, but into longer sequences (chapters) with beginnings and endings of their own. One begins a new chapter by settling in a new town, beginning a career, entering a relationship, giving birth, or in general by undertaking a major task or initiating a sequence of events with an anticipated outcome of whatever kind. These new beginnings resound more or less deeply within the self, sometimes profoundly, sometimes scarcely penetrating the surface of our being. When it resonates deeply, a new beginning typically marks a fundamental change in direction or orientation, a transformation in which something must be left behind in anticipation of something that is to come. What is left behind may itself be grieved, occasionally with an intensity equal to that which accompanies death.

For every beginning, naturally, there is an ending. Every significant ending is an intimation of the final end that is death, and sometimes it is experienced as such. As philosopher Paul Tillich writes: "Every end that we experience in nature and mankind says to us in a loud voice, 'You also will come to an end!' It may reveal itself in the farewell to a place where we have lived for a long time, the separation from the fellowship of intimate associates, the death of someone near to us. Or it may become apparent to us in the breakdown of a work which gave meaning to us, the ending of a whole period of life, the approach of old age, or even in the melancholy side of nature visible in the autumn."[17]

The end of childhood, youth, and middle age each foreshadow one's personal death, as do the endings of all the chapters or phases of one's life. But perhaps most of all, the loss of someone close announces in the plainest terms our personal mortality. This "partial death" is not only a foreshadowing of what is to come, but is experienced, as this term suggests, as the death of another and, simultaneously, of an aspect of oneself. This remarkable phenomenon of double mourning, in which not only the deceased is grieved but that which the deceased symbolically represented within the self, is among the most arresting, and potentially undermining, experiences of human life. What it suggests, disturbing as it may sound, is that ultimately it is for ourselves that we grieve.

17

Public death. A few die very public deaths. As I write this, a man who was my native country's most eminent public figure of the past century has died. In life, Pierre Trudeau was both celebrated and reviled, a man who mobilized a nation by a conception of justice all his own. In death, this formidable man becomes still more a public figure, a symbol of a nation come of age and an ideal of what we might become.

The death of someone who was a great public figure, no matter how intensely private his later life became, marks the transition of an individual from a vital contributor to a nation's affairs to a symbol that may endure through the ages. In death George Washington is not merely a man, an accomplished general and statesman, but represents the spirit of a young and defiant nation determined to chart its own course. Napoleon in death is not only a revolutionary and an emperor, but an enduring symbol of the confidence and exuberance of a nation. At the opposite extreme, Adolf Hitler in death symbolizes for all time the evil of which human beings are capable.

Privately, there is nothing that distinguishes the death of a great public figure from that of the rest of us. One faces death, after all, not as a public figure but as an individual alone with one's fate. Yet publicly, as the phenomenon of mass mourning demonstrates, the death of such an individual can take on mythic proportions. An enduring symbol is born in the death of a man, a symbol that is at long last the property of a nation now that the man is no longer here to tamper with the image we have made of him. Were public figures now deceased to return from the grave to behold the images and the symbols that we have fashioned in their likeness (yet for purposes entirely our own), how likely is it that they would perceive any resemblance between the persons they were and the symbols they have become?

18

What is death? Physicians, psychologists, and philosophers often define death by distinguishing it into several varieties: clinical death, brain death, psychological death, civil death, social death, anthropological death, and many others besides. What they have in common is a certain deprivation of life or vitality, a ceasing to exist as the being one was. Anthropological death, for example, refers to the splitting off of an individual from the group or community to which one had belonged, in which one had gained an identity and an orientation. Social death is characterized by complete withdrawal from interpersonal relationships, usually in anticipation of physical death, accompanied often by an absence of hope and a sense of incapacity. In each of its forms, death is conceived as a negation, a state of being cut off irrevocably from a prior condition of "life" or well-being.

That death is defined in oppositional terms — as essentially a negation or antithesis of something else — would suggest that those persons described as "living" have no part of death, that we are separated from death as if by an abyss. However, what concepts such as social, civil, and anthropological death suggest, albeit indirectly, is that life and death may not be altogether opposite phenomena, that the issue of their relation is more complex and subtle than traditionally conceived. There are perhaps degrees of death, processes of dying as well as of being recalled to life, and nether regions in which we are suspended between life and death. Among these nether regions is a condition known as psychological death, which can precede clinical death by a considerable period. This is a condition in which one not only loses touch with life, but loses all awareness of one's being. As such, it is a form of unconsciousness, yet one not categorically unlike the forgetfulness of life into which so many of the living fall.

To live is to live as a member of a given species, with a particular mode of awareness or a sense of how to negotiate an environment. It is not only to bear a certain physiology and psychology, but to possess a mode of consciousness appropriate to a given species.

In the case of human beings, consciousness is not only more differ-
entiated and complex than that of other species, it is also to a considerable degree a matter of choice. We determine at every moment
the objects on which our awareness will rest as well as the degree of
attention we will pay to them. With consciousness comes not only
the reassurance that we have understood, and can therefore cope
with, objects in our world, but also anxiety about our own existence in that world. Anxiety and uncertainty are suppressed by
means of a more general suppression of consciousness itself, and by
this means alone. The condition of anxiety belongs to human existence not accidentally, but essentially. Our distaste for anxiety and
for all that is related to it — including suffering, insecurity, and uncertainty — regularly prompts us to flee not only from these states
but from what underlies them all — consciousness itself. We adopt
a willful unconsciousness of life as a form of protection against
death.

This is the forgetfulness of life to which I have referred above.
While it is not a form of death, including psychological death, neither is it what one could call participation in life, but something
suspended, as it were, somewhere between the two. It is in this condition of forgetfulness, I would suggest, that most of us spend the
major portion of our lives, prompting the question posed earlier in
this chapter: is it really life that we seek, or the security that alienates us from life?

CHAPTER 2

THE FORGETFULNESS OF LIFE

19

The flight from solitude. Anticipating one's death and grieving the loss of another are occasions that call upon us to turn away from the affairs and distractions of everyday life and to retreat into the inner depths of the self. Like any effective retreat, it is a temporary condition of solitude and introspection, one that makes it possible to emerge fully restored and changed from the experience. Whether such a retreat takes outward form (a journey, returning to one's birthplace or a place where one spent one's youth) or not (moments of private reflection), the imperative to recall oneself confronts us with some force in the encounter with death. The difficulty and complexity of this task are considerable, indeed. How we comport ourselves in the face of death is generally indicative of how we encounter life — authentically or inauthentically, honestly or evasively, with maturity or without it. Neither of these twin tasks — reconciling ourselves with death and with life — is remotely simple in its own terms, yet modern culture conspires in several ways to make these tasks more difficult still.

The first of these is the nearly pathological fear of solitude that pervades modern culture. The positive value of inwardness, solitude, and private reflection virtually disappear in a culture dominated by conformity, outward appearances, and noise. While the fear of loneliness is certainly not peculiar to modern times, the fever pitch it appears to have reached indicates nothing good with respect to the predominating temper of our age. Whatever its causes, the flight from solitude that we now observe extends well beyond a mild fear of loneliness to an unhealthy dread of the interior regions of the personality. As Rollo May has observed: "Is it not too much to say that modern man, sensing his own inner hollowness, is afraid that if he should not have his regular associates around him, should not have the talisman of his daily program and his routine of work, if he should forget what time it is, that he would feel, though in an inarticulate way, some threat like that which one experiences on the brink of psychosis? When one's customary ways of orienting oneself are threatened, and one is without other selves around one, one is thrown back on inner resources and inner strength, and this is what modern people have neglected to develop. Hence loneliness is a real, not imaginary, threat to many of them."[18] If it is socially permissible to enjoy solitude on occasion as an escape from a more usual condition of gregariousness, and then for short periods of time, it is decidedly out of step with modern culture to do so on a regular basis, and positively indecent if for its own sake. People who enjoy solitude for more than brief durations are, we commonly say, antisocial, eccentric, and likely deviant. Their solitude is "misinterpreted," as Nietzsche put it, "as a flight from reality"[19] and a symptom of social ineptitude since, according to most, it is in gregariousness alone that human life consists. This is a life and a gregariousness in the midst of which nothing quite comes into focus, in which silence is menacing and loneliness dreaded.

The main defense against such loneliness is, of course, social acceptance, a value of infinite price in modern culture. Total absorption in the group — be it our social circle, family, church, or community in general — becomes our chief pastime, and conformity to it our first principle. Even when professing individualism, the individualism we commonly practice is a counterfeit form, resembling in its conformity and dread of solitude the "herd mentality" of which Nietzsche spoke in the most derisive terms. This is a psychology of absolute conformity to the ways of the group, even when it is disguised (as it frequently is) behind a philosophy of individualism. Lacking a developed sense of personal identity or other inner resources to sustain it, this mentality seeks total immersion in the collective as its main source of identity. The price it demands of the individual is that he not stray from the group in any fashion, including by means of the cultivation of inner depths which would make all conformity unnecessary and temper the fear of loneliness.

Seeking to explain why it is that human beings appear so ready to abandon individual judgment and responsibility the moment they enter a collective unit, Freud proposed the view that in forming a group the herd instinct quickly comes to the fore since the individual senses an opportunity to regress to a condition of childhood dependency, a drive that remains with us throughout life. At the level of the unconscious, Freud maintained, the individual wishes to obey uncritically the figure of the omnipotent parent, represented by the group leader, and to abandon the individual ego, a wish that in adulthood is readily fulfilled by functioning in groups. If Freud's analysis of group psychology is at least partially accurate, one qualification I would add is that the conformity we most often observe today resembles less subordination to an identifiable group leader — a Napoleon or a Hitler demanding blind obedience — than to the invisible authority of public opinion. This is an authority that is everywhere and yet nowhere. It pervades modern culture in its entirety and governs us all while remaining perfectly anonymous and out of reach. Individuals obey it, pollsters seek it out, politicians sing hymns to it, yet it has no center or substance to it, being nothing but an abstract composite of us all. As an abstract idea, it exists only in our imagination or consciousness of it, even as we submit to its dictates.

The plain absurdity of submission to a power that is not only unseen but abstract, consisting precisely of everyone's opinion but one's own, is strangely lost on most of us most of the time. Why this is so, Freud's analysis goes some way toward explaining; however, the obsession with social approval and the flight from solitude seem to require further explanation than psychoanalysis provides. The dread of isolation, and the compulsiveness of the defenses against it, suggest not only an urge to return to the dependency of childhood but an absence of inner resources and capacities of self-direction. Since death represents to us a condition of ultimate aloneness, it is no surprise that we should seek to ignore it at all costs.

20

Cultivating unconsciousness. Nietzsche maintained that at the level of the unconscious, we are all psychologists, capable of the most acute perception into human affairs both personal and interpersonal. Yet in modern culture we actively cultivate unconsciousness of the more vital dimensions of human existence. Most of our lives are spent in a haze of unreflectiveness, a self-imposed obliviousness to the truth of our condition. This avoidance of perception pertains not only to death and the darker side of human existence, but to all matters beneath the surface of everyday life.

How is it that in modern culture this most psychological animal is readily transformed into its virtual opposite — a being of unfocussed sensibilities and muted perception? How did it come to pass that the individual became alienated from itself, from other persons and life itself, and what are the outward manifestations of this phenomenon?

Consider as a case in point the familiar and singularly modern experience of walking through a shopping mall. Each of the hundreds of individuals we encounter possesses a personal history, and all have their experiences and dominant passions inscribed in their features; their successes and failures are apparent in their physical carriage and posture. They express without words the story of a life, their characteristic choices and willful evasions displaying a level of intensity and vitality, a socio-economic status, and an unrepeatable individuality. Every feature and gesture demonstrates a yearning for visibility. We need not be trained psychologists to perceive any of this since every person we encounter has gone far out of his way, intentionally or unintentionally, to make himself unambiguous to us. Consider further the myriad sights and sounds that practically assault the senses, the enormous array of lights, consumer goods, voices, music, and advertisements everywhere we turn. These too tell a story. The item we have purchased may have been manufactured under the most brutal conditions, the music we hear may have skyrocketed its performer to the pinnacle of fame while being devoid of creativity or sincerity, and the businesses we patronize may be products of lifetimes of effort. Yet, attend to any of these things we do not, in our hasty preoccupation with carrying out our daily affairs.

Conditions of modern life seem to demand a strategic avoidance of perception, an unconsciousness that goes beyond what is necessary for action. It is well known that an excess of reflection can inhibit human action, just as indiscriminate perception is a barrier to focused understanding. Attention is necessarily selective; however, the refusal of perception to which I refer well exceeds what is necessary for action. There is a deeper purpose served in the cultivation of unconsciousness, an unspoken and widely shared determination to ignore our own interiors.

21

Turning our backs on life. In turning away from ourselves we turn away from life itself in its more profound aspects. The better part of life is spent skimming its surface, fearing that should we penetrate to any depth we shall encounter something terrifying, some inner abyss that we must not look upon. As a consequence, we consume our energies in anything that enables us to gain control, to put the mind at ease, and to convince ourselves that the surface aspect of life is its only aspect.

We immerse ourselves in the practical, the habitual, and the commonplace in nearly everything we do, even while sensing (or struggling not to sense) that our existence must contain some deeper significance than that which claims the larger share of our energies. We become caught up in a bustle of activity centered around making money, spending money, and enhancing our reputation. When not caught up in the rat race, we seek diversions in the form of leisure and entertainment, activities that we continually seek, but which themselves are often distractions of the most trivial sort. Even those who pride themselves on eluding the rat race of production and consumption — such as many academics, for example — typically fall into a rat race of a different kind: the race for reputation and position.

In any case, we turn our backs on life and on our own inner depths by the same means. In their place we substitute distractions and the pursuit of outward respectability in whatever form yields the greatest pleasure or is most readily achieved. Almost invariably, being well thought of is the ultimate standard and purpose of our actions rather than any end that resonates more deeply within the self.

22

The existential vacuum. When Nietzsche announced the "death of God" over a century ago, he was proclaiming not only the demise of the Judeo-Christian religion but, more significantly, the loss of an absolute standard of values. Modern culture had lost its moral center as had the modern individual, who had now to fashion his or her own standard of values since he (and she) could no longer look to an objective or universal measure to orient human existence. The death of God meant that the individual was now thrown back on its own resources, a task that religion had always spared it by herding it into a collective unit and placing itself in authority over it.

At the present time, with all forms of authoritarianism in apparent decline together with many traditional worldviews, the general unease and disorientation of which Nietzsche spoke remains with us, if it has not evidently increased. Psychologist Victor Frankl observes that "every age has its own collective neurosis," and he says that it is the "existential vacuum which is the mass neurosis of the present time."[20]

What Nietzsche called "nihilism" — literally, the belief in nothing (*nihil*), but in Nietzsche's usage a broader phenomenon of malaise and meaninglessness brought on by the collapse of the Platonic-Judeo-Christian worldview — finds expression within individual psychology in an inner void or sense that one's life lacks ultimate significance. This widespread psychological phenomenon, according to Frankl, is attributable to two causes, one ancient and one modern.[21] The first is the loss by early humans of fundamental instincts which had previously determined behavior more or less automatically, a loss that compelled human beings to choose how they would live and act. The second is the loss in modern times of traditions which had long provided us with a worldview and a morality that expressed a sense of the ultimate meaning of human life. Once again, we are faced with a loss that decenters our existence and compels us to identify a new source of meaning by our own lights. We are "forced to be free" and uncertain how to proceed. The main symptom of the existential vacuum, Frankl maintains, is less anxiety or distress than boredom. It is a consuming boredom and purposelessness that leads us into abject conformity with public opinion or with others' expectations. It is a boredom that reaches into the depths of the personality and admits of no simple cure, the only lasting remedy being a self-chosen identity and a purpose for one's existence.

May has similarly described a condition of ennui and emptiness as pervasive in modern times, a condition he as well traces to the collapse of traditions and of a "center of values" by which to orient our lives. Its loss, while a necessary step in the transition from psychological immaturity to maturity, at the same time creates a profound upheaval in the transition from one manner of living to another. This is a transition (at once philosophical, moral, and psychological) from a way of life that had appeared certain and absolute to one that recognizes the contingency of all things and the inescapability of human freedom. It is a transition that is fraught with anxiety since the individual must now draw upon inner resources in choosing a way of life rather than appeal to the authority of tradition — resources that are often underdeveloped. In consequence, many people experience a general "feeling of emptiness or vacuity" along with a sense of being "powerless to do anything effective about their lives or the world they live in."[22] Often stemming from this as well is an incapacity to make decisions or to identify what one wishes or feels, an inability that again prompts us into conformity with public opinion.

If at the "center" of our being, or the innermost reaches of the self, lies emptiness only, it would seem that we are faced with two options. Either we may look "outward," to tradition, authority, or public opinion for a standard by which to live and act, or "within" for a standard of our own choosing or invention. The former option is undoubtedly the more common, and the easier, of the two, despite the widely expressed discontent to which it so often gives rise. We have fairly exhausted the resources of ancient traditions, particularly concerning fundamental questions of meaning. As for "public opinion," even its most ardent followers are hard-pressed to provide an account of its considerable authority. Like most forms of authority, its power over us stems mainly from our choice not to examine it or to seek a legitimating rationale.

23

Mass society. The existential vacuum, I would suggest, is intimately related to another fact of modern life, although which is cause and which is effect may be difficult to determine.

This is the phenomenon of mass society which certain existential philosophers (most notably Karl Jaspers and Gabriel Marcel) brought to our attention mainly during the middle decades of the twentieth century. These writers identified the drawbacks of modern social relations, which most often take place on a mass scale. The individual in mass society encounters other persons, particularly in public places, less as individual selves than as an anonymous mass of humanity. Social life on a mass scale is experienced as all but devoid of human significance, other persons being in the main either useful "resources" or obstacles in our path. The life of modern mass society becomes increasingly dominated by rationalization techniques, the identification and administration of the needs of the masses, hyper-regulation and conformity, and by a way of life leveled down to an order of uninspired normality.

The fate of the individual in mass society is described by Jaspers in the following terms: "[T]he time arrived when nothing in the individual's immediate and real environing world was any longer made, shaped, or fashioned by that individual for his own purposes; when everything that came, came merely as the gratification of momentary need, to be used up and cast aside; when the very dwelling-place was machine-made, when the environment had become despiritualised, when the day's work grew sufficient to itself and ceased to be built up into a constituent of the worker's life — then man was, as it were, bereft of his world."[23] The individual becomes increasingly identified with a function — primarily an economic function which serves the social whole — as its very existence and identity are dominated by values of production and consumption. Individuality disappears into functionality, demographics, statistical norms or, in a word, the mass. While opportunities for personal expression and difference grow ever fewer, along with all but the most adolescent forms of rebellion, these very qualities paradoxically become the more prized as opportunities for their expression diminish. Rebellion and individuality are admired so long as they are confined to stage and screen, to entertainment figures, or otherwise pushed to the sidelines of ordinary life. As if yearning nostalgically for what we have lost, we reserve our deepest admiration for individuals who stand out from the mass while devoting our energies to appearing as inconspicuous as possible.

Once again, it is the quest for security that motivates this form or manifestation of the forgetfulness of life. One becomes absorbed in the mass not for any profound riches it may offer, but to gain outward respectability, to make a living, to get along with one's neighbors, to avoid friction, and to make one's life easy, predictable, and unobjectionable. We embrace conformity not as an end in itself but as the necessary price of security and comfort in their various forms.

As survival and respectability become the central purposes of human existence, a deeper participation in life becomes increasingly difficult and the existential vacuum within the self appears to widen. Yet the pressures of mass society would shape both our outward actions and our private inclinations and identity according to a uniform pattern, one dominated by values of survival, security, and ease. Living becomes a stereotyped result of pressures experienced daily via television, the press, popular entertainment, advertising, and a variety of institutions, pressures that urge us to fashion ourselves after a common pattern. Through a complex system of rewards and punishments both subtle and unsubtle, the capacity to stand out from the environment is unlearned, even as we privately long for something — a political leader, an entertainment figure, a distant memory — to remind us of what we have lost.

24

Nostalgia and rootlessness. A tree does not reach the heights unless its roots reach deep into the earth. Yet rootlessness is an increasingly pervasive fact of modern life. While we yearn nostalgically for small spaces and towns of "human scale," we live increasingly in cities whose most pronounced characteristics are largeness, anonymity, sameness, and a near-total removal from nature. The things we habitually choose very often are the opposite of that for which our spirits yearn — rural life, small towns, proximity to nature, life on a scale that fosters serenity and intimacy. Witness the phenomenon of the contemporary suburban home, identical to its neighbors yet furnished with mementos and pictures on the walls that capture scenes of rural simplicity, nature, olden times, or another symbolic representation of what we have left behind in the quest for security and respectability. The cottage on the lake is where we visit; the house in the city is where we live. Quiet reflection is for Sunday mornings; the rest of the week is for getting ahead.

25

Rationalization. There is nothing supremely valuable or irreplaceable about the individual who has disappeared into a function, still less into a demographic norm, an instance of the general mass. Under conditions of modern culture, social life bears vitally not on the individual but on the general, the collective, the norm. It is broad socio-economic indicators and statistics that prompt political institutions to action, not the conditions of individual lives.

In contemporary politics, it is not whether the people are free that matters most, but whether they are well fed, secure, and slow to complain. It is as if in modern democracies we had agreed that since we have lost any vital connection with life, ourselves, and each other, we may at least be well provided for, with programs and institutions designed to meet all our needs as efficiently as possible. If we are without inner depths, we may as well become content with the surface of life, acting at a level of stimulus and response, reward and punishment. We need not worry whether we are free, for we are unsure what we would do with our freedom except seek as much opportunity for distraction as possible.

Vaclav Havel, one of the more astute political observers of recent times, writes that modern political culture is at a crossroads between what he calls the "post-totalitarian" system of government — one dominated not by an all-powerful ruler, but by an all-powerful system to which all must conform and which all must serve — and a political order premised on "the aims of life." "Between the aims of the post-totalitarian system and the aims of life there is a yawning abyss: while life, in its essence, moves towards plurality, diversity, independent self-constitution and self-organization, in short, towards the fulfillment of its own freedom, the post-totalitarian system demands conformity, uniformity, and discipline. While life ever strives to create new and 'improbable' structures, the post-totalitarian system contrives to force life into its most probable states. . . . The essential aims of life are present naturally in every person. In everyone there is some longing for humanity's rightful dignity, for moral integrity, for free expression of being and a sense of transcendence over the world of existence. Yet, at the same time, each person is capable of coming to terms with living within the lie. Each person somehow succumbs to a profane trivialization of his or her inherent humanity, and to utilitarianism."[24]

The utilitarianism Havel mentions is the general approach to social and political issues long characteristic of Western democracies, in which "the greatest happiness of the greatest number" serves as the ultimate criterion of justice and state action. While perhaps unobjectionable on the face of it, utilitarianism as a political creed habitually offers small sacrifices in human freedom and individuality to the mass and its material "needs." These needs become increasingly numerous over time and they demand greater sacrifices of liberty, until the scope of individual freedom diminishes to what statistical norms and majority decisions deem proper — typically the way of life of the mass, and very little besides.

If the utilitarian democracies of the present time value above all the satisfaction of material needs, then as a means necessary to that end they require the introduction of rationalization techniques that can be applied on a system-wide basis. Government must ascertain needs, levy taxes, redistribute income, regulate, and discipline the population in order to meet the requirements of the system with optimal efficiency. Politics becomes an affair of identifying the most rational (that is, efficient) means of achieving ends approved by public opinion, whatever these may be. It is the art not of making people free, but of keeping them quiet.

In such a system, the citizen disappears into the functionary, a unit of political calculation, an asset or a liability, a producer and consumer of utilities. "Justice" increasingly becomes an affair of "distribution" — which groups are to receive which benefits, in what amount, and at whose expense. As politics assumes an essentially mechanistic, bureaucratic form, the people themselves begin to resemble mechanisms, functionaries, and consumers of utilities rather than a free citizenry. In such an order, we risk losing sight of the distinction that philosopher Immanuel Kant drew between the "dignity" of individuals and their mere "value," the latter term being properly applied to things rather than persons. A bearer of dignity transcends all value and all functionality. And, dignity arises from an interiority — a capacity and an integrity — that are found beneath the surface of utilitarian rationality.

26

Hyperstimulation and hyperactivity. The price that we pay for security is one we do not often see. What we immediately perceive are the benefits that security brings — the ease, comfort, and predictability of a lifestyle that, to all appearances, is beyond change. We are not at home in a world of change, contingency, or uncertainty, so we feel compelled to transform it by any means possible to one that affords maximum reassurance that everything is, and will always remain, at our disposal. We seek a respite from struggle, whether because we sense our incapacity to succeed or to find meaning in the attempt.

If we cannot escape the knowledge that everything comes with a price, we would at least prefer not to be reminded of this. Indeed, we would often pay the highest price, and happily, provided it be invisible. Here I am reminded of a bitter political debate that occurred in Canada in the 1980s when the national government introduced a general goods and services tax to replace an older — and hidden — manufacturer's sales tax at little or no additional cost to the taxpayer. The new tax was greeted with bitter disapproval from virtually all segments of the Canadian population; yet it was not the tax itself that prompted popular outrage, but the fact of its visibility.

What peculiarity of human nature impels us to turn our backs resolutely not only on death, on the price we pay for every choice, and other unpleasant realities, but ultimately on life itself? Human beings live in the world by understanding it and, on this basis, making ourselves at home in it. Yet we imagine that we can live under comforting illusions without paying a price or losing a vital connection with life. Intuitively we all sense the enormous price we have paid for the illusion of security, even as we struggle not to.

As if life itself were speaking through us — not directly, but by forcing itself indirectly through subterranean networks of repression, evasion, and falsehood — modern life takes on a neurotic franticness that compels us toward hyperactivity and hyperstimulation. Our lives take on an urgency toward unceasing activity and excitement. The contemporary workplace is a squirrel cage of bustle and activity toward a purpose that lacks any meaningful connection to the life of the employee. The remainder of our time, or a major portion of it, is spent in a frantic quest for excitement and stimulation. Television advertisements assault the eye by flashing a dozen images per second, magazine covers promise sexual titillation without any possibility of consummation or meaning, mainstream news reporting increasingly resembles tabloid entertainment, and politics becomes a show of personalities complete with heroes and villains, plot twists and scandals. Modern life is increasingly dominated by anything that excites, stimulates, or distracts.

If the pace of modern life is one of frantic urgency, such that there is always too much to do and too little time, its focus is almost invariably outer-directed. Our activities are organized around getting what we need, winning approval and staying one step ahead, rather than finding a deeper meaning in our daily activities. What is most remarkable about this is that there is nothing inherently

meaningless in any of these pursuits. Watching a movie can profoundly affect our sense of who we are; the job of laborer can be an
opportunity to experience the satisfaction of physical competence.
Yet our focus often lies exclusively on outward rewards and punishments, on keeping busy and making noise. Beneath our hyperactivity and over-stimulation is an alienation from some firmer ground
within the self. If we can never be still, it is because we have lost
contact with — or failed to create — a semblance of peace which
comes with an understanding of ourselves and the purpose of our
existence.

The quest for security is not "the good life," but a respite from
life. If we would prefer not to perceive this, we are reminded of it
daily in the hyperactivity and hyper-stimulation of modern life.
Both are symptomatic of an alienation from ourselves and from life,
even as life reasserts itself by urging us frantically toward action,
sensation, or any other reminder that we are living beings. As psychoanalysis has long taught, vital energy that does not reach its out-
let by a direct route persists until it finds an alternative, and
emerges from it with an urgency and compulsiveness that may be
profoundly damaging to the personality. It seeks compensation for
what has been repressed or denied, even as we struggle to deny
what is taking place within and without us.

27

Demystification. If it is characteristic of modern life to gravitate
toward outer-directed activity, external appearances, and material-
ity, if we would sooner skim quickly along the surface than plunge
to the depths, the explanation lies partly in what we fear the depths

hold for us. If we sense an existential vacuum within, what we en-counter without is a universe stripped of meaning and demystified by modern science and philosophy. Religious worldviews of old had invested the cosmos with human significance. The heavens were populated by deities profoundly concerned with the human world below, deities of great mystery and supreme authority. Everything in the universe had its rightful place, every person an assigned role, every life a hope for a personal victory over death. Human beings inhabited an enchanted world of saints and demons, forces of good and evil between which one must urgently take sides. We lived in accordance with meanings writ large in the heavens and out of a spiritual and moral center within.

These worldviews were replaced in modern times by scientific explanations and philosophical skepticism of practically everything that had come before. We now have no reason to believe in an un-seen world, no proof of an afterlife, and no center from which to live. The human world, we realize, is not the center of the universe, our species was not created from nothing, the conscious ego is not firmly installed atop the unconscious. Our nation is not the center of civilization, nor is our culture supreme in its achievements. In short, we are not special except in ways that, through our own ef-forts, we create.

These sobering truths are now commonly accepted, yet the profound psychological loss they occasion is easily underestimated. There is something in the human spirit that forever wishes to stand out, and to live on the basis of a meaning connected with our mode of standing out. Even as we conform outwardly, privately we remain convinced of our cosmic specialness and would safeguard this conviction at any price. Our nation may not be the center of known civilization, but it is unrivaled in its political institutions, economic power, and military prowess. Our hometown may bear a striking resemblance to many others, but it possesses an unmistakable character and charm found nowhere else. It is no wonder so many famous people come from there.

If modern science and philosophy have all but completely banished mystery and cosmic specialness from the universe, they fly often to the opposite extreme. Sacred mysteries of old are now mechanical operations knowable and predictable in every detail. The celestial sky is now a cold universe of complete indifference to human affairs. Even romantic love and the sexual act have been demythologized to become merely so many biochemical processes and bodily functions. Modern science has no power to enchant; it merely explains. Science accents the logical, the causal, and the repeatable. The victories it has gained over medieval systems of belief are by no means to be regretted, yet for all its capacity to explain what is, modern science cannot (nor does it seek to) invest the universe with meaning. Science demystifies, debunks, and describes; and where science cannot play that role, modern philosophy has done so. Yet if just about everything has now been demystified and demythologized, we face a task of no little difficulty which lies well beyond the scope of modern science.

This is to reinvest existence in one fashion or another with meaning. If the physical universe is no longer conceivable as the abode of the gods, at least the universe of human affairs may be conceived as one of significance. It is, after all, not existence in general that ultimately concerns us, but human existence. What is the meaning of this in a universe that in itself is without meaning? How do we create significance and cosmic specialness after the death of God?

28

Public life. "In solitude," writes philosopher Jose Ortega y Gasset, "man is his truth; in society, he tends to be his mere conventionality or falsification. The genuine reality of human living includes the duty of frequent withdrawal to the solitary depths of oneself."[25] The imperative toward private withdrawal is among the principal obligations each of us owes to ourselves. Yet if one encounters an existential vacuum in "the solitary depths of oneself," one often flies in the direction of outward things and public life. We become outer-directed beings, avoiding solitude and cultivating unconsciousness of the most ultimate things. It is understandable that we would do so, given the profound unpleasantness of realizing that our hidden depths contain an emptiness we do not know how to fill.

Yet what do we encounter when we turn away from the self and toward the world of public life? We direct our gaze to the heavens and find a cold and indifferent universe. We turn our attention to the public domain and find a mass society and social institutions that often seem less interested in the persons they serve than in their own well-being. If politics as "public service" appears a thing of the past, so too does "community" (as many in the "communitarian" movement have lamented) or even genuine civility. One increasingly finds in public spaces a notable lack of civility, an impersonalness, and a hostility that makes it difficult to recognize oneself and to make oneself at home in public life. Given the choice, we would all wish to recognize ourselves in the institutions and communities that surround us, to be visible and at home outside the private sphere. Yet what we find instead is the mass, a thousand faces we have never encountered before and will never encounter again, a restless bustle of activity that is forever getting in our way and we in its.

It is no mystery that communitarians, nationalists, and many others who are politically inclined yearn nostalgically for a time in the past (real or imagined) when a greater semblance of community existed, or when public life remained on a "human scale." Nostalgia is always foolish; it is no more possible to return to a time prior to mass civilization than to rehabilitate pre-modern systems of belief. Yet if modernity is here to stay, might it still be hoped that public life could be a site of meaning? If there are simply too many of us, with too little in common, to reinstate the ideal of "community," might we fashion institutions that make possible a greater degree of civility than what we currently find? Must it only be "in solitude," as Gasset expressed it, that "man is his truth," or might we create conditions that enable us to be ourselves and at home in public places, as we imagine (or perhaps fantasize) was once the case?

What would make it possible for the individual in mass society to be, if not cosmically special, then at least visible, civil, and free? A common answer is for political institutions to yield almost indiscriminately to those vocal segments of the population that claim a special right to some benefit or other, usually on grounds of their having been victimized by some other group or by an unkind fate. As we now observe, this idea leads directly to the proverbial scramble for the loaves and fishes, with more and more groups effectively competing for special favor from the state, and to a further deterioration of the civility of public life. A better answer will have to be found than the politics of special interests, or the nostalgia for "community." Whatever the complete answer to this question would be, its accent would necessarily lie with the individual and with the conditions of social life that make it possible for each of us to be equal participants in a free society.

Even here, however, we shall not find a full solution to the problem described. If it is the private task of each of us to fashion meaning within our own lives, it is our public and political task to create a semblance of meaning in our institutions — a public meaning, to be sure, yet one that is capable of resonating to a modest depth within the individual self.

29

Life in three dimensions. While life itself may be three-dimensional, typically we do not live in three dimensions, but in one or two. Plato famously depicted human nature as divided into three components — reason, spirit, and body — and argued that all persons are naturally disposed to exhibit one of these in a predominant fashion. When we examine the lives that most of us lead, it appears that Plato may well have been correct. The life of the scholar, artist, or blue-collar worker typically manifests one dimension of human "nature" or existence to an almost absurd degree. The scholar lives a deliberately cloistered existence, often totally removed from what the rest of the human race calls "the real world." At the opposite extreme, the blue-collar worker may lead what the scholar contemp-

tuously calls the unexamined life — one in which thought is entirely restricted to the practical affairs of everyday life. Yet, however
connected the laborer may be to his or her physicality, the scholar to
rationality, or the artist to the realm of spirit, we seldom encounter
those connected with life in all three of its dimensions.

Plato undoubtedly misrepresents human nature in portraying
it as an object of fixed necessity. There is absolutely no basis in observation for the view of human nature or life as necessarily limited
to one- or perhaps two-dimensionality. Unusual as it may be for human beings to be in touch with life in its intellectual, spiritual, and
physical dimensions, the fact of that rarity is fully explicable in
terms of the choices we make. We choose our roles only to become
them — subsequently forgetting that these are indeed choices,
choices that could have been otherwise but that, once taken, begin
to dominate our existence. We become disconnected from that
which is not strictly enjoined by our roles or our station in life. If an
engine possessed six cylinders but fired on only two, would we not
say that the engine suffered from a deficiency? And yet the prohibition against intellectual matters prevalent among blue-collar labor-
ers is matched by an equally absurd prohibition among intellectuals
against the realm of the physical. A factory worker would no sooner
pick up a book of philosophy than a member of our professorate
would take up weightlifting.

30

The institutionalization of birth and death. We are born and we die
in institutions. If we are unlucky, we spend a great part of our lives
there as well. The classic deathbed scene in which the dying person

imparts wisdom and perhaps a final blessing or request to the living has now been replaced by a decidedly clinical affair dominated by technology and the medical profession. If the human being is conceived as a mechanism, then death is the failure of that mechanism, and often a failure as well for the physician charged with his or her care. Death is the final adversary, to be combated by an institutional and technological apparatus that practically dwarfs the event of death itself. The dying person is isolated from the world, from home, and often from relatives as well. Terminal patients' awareness of what is happening to them is often obscured by drugs, at a time when they may urgently desire to keep their wits about them.

To be sure, there is nothing sinister in any of this, as least as it concerns the motives of the great majority of medical professionals. Their aim is to keep patients alive, and when feasible they will go to extraordinary lengths to do so. One would not wish this otherwise, yet the modern institutionalization of death also brings with it a certain dehumanization. As the terminally ill are swept up into the apparatus of the modern hospital, their deaths do not entirely belong to them, but in a sense to the institutional and technological apparatus itself. Close relatives and even patients become passive spectators of a process that is often beyond their comprehension or power to control. As poet Rainer Maria Rilke eloquently writes, "The desire to have a death of one's own is becoming more and more rare. In a short time it will be as rare as a life of one's own."[26] Dying is a process and a task that calls us to engage our faculties rather than to surrender them, or our autonomy, to a physician or institution whose agenda may well conflict with that of the patient.

Dying patients may wish to die at home, under conditions or at a time of their choosing. They may wish to die in peace without extraordinary, or even ordinary, measures to prolong their existence. As the hospice movement, "right to die" activism, and the growing interest in assisted suicide make evident, there is increasing recognition of the limits of medical institutionalization. So long as the dying are denied either an honest prognosis or a final say over their manner of treatment, they are transformed into dehumanized subjects whose deaths are not their own. It may be of ultimate importance to the physician to postpone patients' deaths as long as possible rather than to ensure that their deaths "belong" to them, but the patients' priority may be the reverse. Whatever the patients' wishes in this connection, respecting their dignity clearly entails their right to make determinations of this nature over the recommendations of medical professionals.

31

Life, death, and philosophy. If there were an exception in any field of endeavor or study to the phenomenon I have described as the forgetfulness of life, an exception to Dostoyevsky's remark that "we have all lost touch with life," one would expect to find it in the field of investigation that is philosophy. From its (Western) inception in ancient Greece, philosophy is traditionally defined as the love (*philia*) of wisdom (*sophia*), where "wisdom" refers to knowledge of matters of ultimate importance to human life. Philosophy from its ancient beginnings concerns itself not with everyday trivialities, but with first and last things — first principles of being, the good life for human beings, the nature of beauty, knowledge, and truth — including the phenomena of life and death.

So closely, in fact, have the notions of life and death been historically associated with philosophy that philosophy itself has been described since ancient times as a preparation for death. As Socrates, the patron saint of Western philosophy, famously put it: "Ordinary people seem not to realize that those who really apply themselves in the right way to philosophy are directly and of their own accord preparing themselves for dying and death. If this is true, and they have actually been looking forward to death all their lives, it would of course be absurd to be troubled when the thing comes for which they have so long been preparing and looking forward."[27] Philosophers prepare for death — indeed "make dying their profession"[28] — insofar as they anticipate the release of the soul from the body, a separation that makes it possible for the soul to behold reality in its true dimension, without the distorting influence of the body and the senses. Since, for Socrates, the soul not only survives the death of the body but is able in death to gain pure knowledge of being, a properly philosophical attitude toward death is to welcome it as a liberation from the body as well as to accept it as an inevitability. This attitude toward death Socrates himself demonstrated, facing his own demise with an acceptance and resolve that transformed his death into a symbol of the philosophical life.

Since Socrates's time, death and life have remained central topics of philosophical concern. In the latter nineteenth and early twentieth centuries in particular, these subjects became especially prominent in the writings of existential philosophers (most notably Soren Kierkegaard, Friedrich Nietzsche, Martin Heidegger, Karl Jaspers, Gabriel Marcel, Albert Camus, Jose Ortega y Gasset, and Jean-Paul Sartre). This loosely affiliated group sought to deepen our understanding of human existence and death in a variety of ways, and with much success. Heidegger, for instance, accurately observed that human existence is a "being toward death," or that it invariably contains an anticipation, however implicit, of one's personal death. This anticipation is no merely curious piece of information regarding the distant future, but fundamentally orients our present manner of living. Camus as well writes that "There is but one truly serious philosophical problem, and that is suicide. Judging whether life is or is not worth living amounts to answering the fundamental question of philosophy."[29]

During the last several decades, however, these core topics of philosophy have all but disappeared from view. While in a sense all philosophy is a "philosophy of life," the concept of life itself has been consigned to the sidelines of contemporary academic philosophy. It is sometimes contained within technical terms such as "lifeworld" or "forms of life," but as one observer has noted, "organic life itself — biological life or nature — has been largely discredited or, rather, has come to be seen as irrelevant to questions of meaning and culture."[30] As this most radical field of investigation became absorbed into the academic profession, philosophy came to occupy an increasingly mainstream position in the modern university. The classical "love of wisdom" became yet another branch of the academic industry, to the point where the majority of professional philosophers at the present time would likely be embarrassed to call themselves lovers of wisdom. Lovers of reputation, perhaps; lovers of tenure, absolutely; but lovers of wisdom?

Ortega y Gasset is well within his rights in observing: "To the shame of philosophers it must be said that they have never seen the radical phenomenon that is our life. They have always turned their backs on it, and it has been the poets and novelists, but above all the 'ordinary man,' who has been aware of it with its modes and situations."[31] These are harsh words, and important exceptions do exist, yet one can hardly escape the impression that contemporary philosophy has largely forgotten life and death in its fascination with small technical disputes and micro-issues of no obvious connection to a larger understanding of the human condition. Ortega's suggestion that it is poets, novelists, and "the ordinary man" who best understand life, rather than the modern professor of philosophy, is, in my view, indisputable.

32

Death and contemporary philosophy. If Socrates was right to speak of philosophy as, in a sense, a preparation for death, then we have become ill-prepared indeed. Philosophy, by its nature, makes its home in the abstract world of theory, principles, and rationality, while life and death belong to the concrete order of practice, passion, and nature. It is characteristic of philosophy to investigate particular aspects of the practical or natural order from the standpoint of theory. Despite the negative connotation the word "theory" has received within much of modern culture, there is nothing untoward about the philosophical preoccupation with theory. Indeed, it is precisely by fashioning theories that an explicit understanding of a given object or phenomenon is often gained. Ultimately, it is the bearing that theory has on practice that establishes its value, even when this is limited to comprehending in explicit terms an object, practice, or concept that can be understood by no other means.

While the disdain many feel toward all matters described as "merely theoretical" may be mistaken, it remains that some theoretical investigations bear more directly and vitally on concrete matters of practice than others. Theorizing, be it scientific or philosophical, can radically overhaul our understanding of the most pressing issues facing us, while at other times it can lead to dead ends or to pointless squabbles.

Philosophers, historically, have been correct in regarding death as a theoretical problem, the basic idea being that contemplating death provides a clue not only to life, but to the good life for human beings. If academic philosophers of the present time sometimes overlook this, they often overlook as well that death is not *only* a theoretical problem, but an urgently practical, and existential, problem. It engages not only the reasoning intellect but the passionate nature of human beings. It is no simple curiosity or classroom exercise, but one that brings to bear our capacities of emotional awareness, empathy, introspection, and existential decision. Socrates, theorizing on the nature and meaning of death, does so not as a blackboard exercise, but in a cell awaiting execution.

Contrast this with the kinds of questions often asked by contemporary academics: why, for example, do we trouble ourselves at all about death — our future nonexistence — when our past nonexistence troubles us not at all? What is so special about death that we should not equally worry about our having not existed prior to birth? Or, suppose at some future time, or in a world of science fiction, it were possible to reattach a severed head to its body; would the person with the successfully reattached head have been brought back from the dead? Or: if it were medically possible for a dying person with a healthy brain to receive a whole body transplant, would that person be the same person he or she was before the operation, or a different person? And what of the fear of death: is it rational or irrational?

Could anyone who has authentically encountered death seriously entertain such questions? It is astonishing how many academic philosophers possess the singular capacity to transform matters of the most profound urgency and significance into cute puzzles. Even suicide has been transformed in recent years from what Camus called "the fundamental question of philosophy" into yet another academic exercise. The existential question of life or death in the face of suffering now turns upon the identification of formal criteria of rational decision-making: is suicide a rational or irrational choice? How can we tell? What principles enable us to pronounce with authority the conditions under which suicide is an advisable ("well grounded") or inadvisable course of action? One would not, after all, choose personal destruction if it meant violating sound principles of reasoning, would one?

Consider as a case in point a recent book on the philosophy of suicide. The specific question the author takes up is whether "preemptive suicide," defined as suicide by aging persons that is based on the anticipation of future decline and suffering, rather than present suffering, "can be a fully warranted course of action, the deliberation and enactment of which meet established standards of sound reasoning."[32] The author sets himself the task of identifying several criteria on the basis of which suicide can be allowed to pass as a rational action. The purpose of identifying these criteria, however, is not to offer counsel to individuals actively contemplating suicide — criteria that would undoubtedly go in one ear and out the other — but to judge their action after the fact. As he writes: "[W]e aren't willing to accept how people feel as sufficient to judge their self-destruction rational. . . . [T]he issue here is whether we are prepared to judge suicide or preemptive suicide rational, not whether or not we should intervene in the commission of suicide. . . . [T]here may be cases where we shouldn't intervene in suicide even if we judge it irrational. My concern is to establish the criterial rationality of suicide in general and of preemptive suicide in particular, not to lay down rules for dealing with people considering self-destruction."[33] As if the philosopher's role were that of Monday morning quarterback, this exercise in theory construction involves an intentional removal from the world of practice and of actual life. What conceivable difference does it make, and to whom, if particular acts of suicide are deemed rational or irrational? The only answer that makes sense is that should we determine that certain cases of suicide are irrational, then we would have cause to intervene in one manner or other to prevent those acts from happening. Apart from the issue of intervention — be it in the form of legal intervention by the state or simply well-intentioned advice to persons contemplating suicide — the question of rationality or irrationality is irrelevant.

The forgetfulness of life and death pervades modern culture, including in places — such as academic philosophy — where one would expect it to have been overcome. Yet if it is true that "we have all lost touch with life," exactly what is it with which we have lost touch? In what sense is this the case, and what is the alternative? If most all of modern culture has paid an enormous price for security, convenience, and ease, precisely what is it that we have renounced? If the answer turns upon the concept of "life" — human existence — then what would a more authentic encounter with life be? As I have suggested, we find a clue to this last question in contemplating the meaning of death.

CHAPTER 3
SUICIDE

33

An ancient taboo. Before turning directly to the questions just posed, I wish to examine at some length the issue of voluntary death and the superstitions, both ancient and modern, that surround it. Here again my premise is that investigating death — in this case death by one's own hand — provides a clue to life, or, according to Dostoyevsky's assertion, to that from we have become alienated.

As noted above, Camus has written that the question of suicide, or "whether life is or is not worth living," constitutes "the fundamental question of philosophy." While I would largely agree with that sentiment, there is one qualification that I would introduce in speaking of suicide as a "question of philosophy." Philosophical questions typically have, or seek, one answer that, if not definitively true, represents at the very least the most plausible candidate to emerge from the general discussion to date, an answer that is henceforth permitted to stand as true. Philosophers have long sought the truth in the sense of abstract propositions that agree with factual states of affairs, statements with which we can rest secure and which we need not re-examine, except perhaps for theoretical purposes. Yet in the case of suicide we are faced with both a philosophical and an existential issue, one originating not from any blackboard exercise or semantic puzzle but from their furthest extreme: the existential condition of the individual human being. It is an issue for which we have no reason to believe there exists a single "true" or authoritative answer. In the issue before us, "whether life is or is not worth living" is not resolved in abstract or general terms, but in terms of the life of the one posing the question.

That the answer, therefore, is a contingency flies so directly in the face of tradition that we must address the matter of the ancient taboo against suicide which persists largely unabated to this day. In the Western world, the traditional Christian view has it that suicide is invariably evil, the moral equivalent of murder, the sole difference being that it is oneself, rather than another, who is its victim. The life of the individual being a gift, and also the property, of the Creator (despite the evident contradiction of these two frequently encountered assertions), it is the Creator alone who may bring that life to an end. In Christian terms, suicide constitutes a moral evil since ultimately the life that one is ending is not one's own. The Christian view replaced older conceptions of suicide that had carried influence in ancient Greek and Roman civilization, views that frequently took a considerably more tolerant stance toward voluntary death. The ancient Stoics in particular regarded death by one's own hand as an act of moral freedom and for this reason as eminently human, even noble, in certain circumstances.

Yet it is the Christian view that has dominated Western thought on the subject until modern times, a view that called for the imposition of religious "penalties" on persons who had committed suicide. These included the refusal of Christian burial rites, the trial of the suicide (represented by the body of the deceased) before a court authorized to try homicide cases, the confiscation of the deceased's assets, and often the "torture" or degradation of the dead body. The modern period saw this view slowly amended, beginning in the eighteenth century when Germany (in 1751) and later France (in 1790) decriminalized suicide, while continuing to regard the act as a moral evil. Other European and North American jurisdictions continued to deem suicide a legal crime until very recent times. England, for example, decriminalized the act only in 1961; Canada in 1972; still others have yet to do so. Aiding and abetting suicide, along with assisted suicide and euthanasia, remain crimes in most Western nations, providing continuing evidence of the disapproval widely felt toward voluntary death.

Yet modern times have also witnessed a partial transformation of suicide from a moral evil and legal crime to a medical problem. The success of psychology, sociology, and the social sciences generally (including in the domain of public policy) ushered in an altogether new view of suicide as a pathological phenomenon, almost invariably a product of mental illness to which the appropriate stance was less one of moral or legal condemnation than the apparently scientific one of explaining its causes and managing its prevention. The assumption remained that there is a truth about suicide which it is the business of government, scientific expertise, and common morality to bring to bear against those individuals who would seriously question whether life is worth living.

Among the moral arguments against suicide are, as mentioned, the Christian belief that God alone (sometimes the state as well) possesses the right of life and death, a view that continues to enjoy broad support. Also popular is the "slippery slope" argument, to the effect that to cease disapproving of suicide is but one step away from approving of such acts as assisted suicide, euthanasia, or even homicide. Once the "sanctity of life" principle is compromised, this argument states, there is no basis on which to condemn any act resulting in the loss of human life. It would, for instance, create a moral pressure upon the elderly to end their lives prematurely so as not to burden financially strapped health care systems, or a pressure on government and the medical profession to lessen their commitment to palliative care or to discovering new cures for fatal diseases. This commonly-cited argument for upholding the suicide taboo is identical to the argument formerly used against legalized contraception; as that argument stated, should we permit individuals to decide freely the timing and circumstances of birth, we would bring about an irreversible decline in the moral fabric of society and erode the sanctity of life.

Still another argument proposes that suicide could never be a rational choice since the very notion of rational choice presupposes the intelligibility of the option under consideration. In the case of suicide, one is unable to gain a clear understanding of the condition one is seeking to bring about, and for this reason cannot rationally evaluate it. One is never in a position to evaluate and contrast the states of being alive and being dead since, obviously, one has not experienced the latter and can therefore not know whether it would further one's real interests. Such interests can only be served in life, the conclusion appears to follow.

Yet important exceptions to the traditional view have existed, including not only the ancient Stoics but such modern philosophers as Nietzsche and David Hume. As Hume expressed it in the eighteenth century, "suicide may often be consistent with interest and with our duty to ourselves"[34]; also, "a man of sixty-five, by dying, cuts off only a few years of infirmities."[35] Nietzsche as well spoke of "the difficult art of — going at the right time"[36]: "Many die too late and some die too early. Still the doctrine sounds strange: 'Die at the right time.'"[37]

My own view on the matter is that while there is a sense in which the question whether life is or is not worth living is a philosophical question, it is not one that we may expect to be answered in general or categorical terms. There are simply too many particularities, contingencies, and qualifications that we would need to consider in order to pronounce a categorical yes or no, contingencies relating to the detailed circumstances of the one posing the question. In the case of such existential issues as the worthwhileness of life, or life or death in the face of profound suffering, each of us is radically free to follow a course of our own choosing, without moral obligations impelling us one way or the other. Defending this view will be my task in this chapter.

34

"*Rational*" *suicide?* While the taboo against suicide remains largely in place at the present time, I am hardly alone in proposing that elective death in some circumstances is an act that calls for respect rather than moral disapproval. Some contemporary philosophers have defended the view not only that one possesses a right to die, but that suicide under certain conditions may be said to be a "rational choice." As noted above, one current debate in philosophical circles bears on the identification of formal criteria which, if met, would qualify a given case of suicide as rational. While many, of course, deny categorically that such criteria exist, or that suicide could ever be a rational course of action, others have defended the possibility of rational suicide.

Most often, those who defend suicide as a rational option focus upon relatively straightforward cases in which terminally-ill individuals, subject to extreme suffering without reasonable hope of remission or improvement in their condition, choose on the basis of firmly held convictions to bring their suffering to an end. Suicidal acts of this kind are often described less as freely chosen courses of action than as effectively coerced by circumstances beyond the patient's, or anyone's, control. Less commonly, suicide in anticipation of certain and irreversible decline is regarded as rational, for instance by C. G. Prado, who is cited in Chapter 2.

That author suggests four criteria for rational suicide; they are that a given case of suicide be "1. Soundly deliberated, *and* 2. Cogently motivated, *and* 3. Prescribed by well-grounded values without undue depreciation or untimely contravention of survival's value, *and* 4. In the agent's best interests."[38] On the face of it, these criteria appear more or less sound to most of us not already committed to a religious worldview. They approximate at the very least a view that is gradually gaining in popularity. The observation I wish to make, however, concerns more fundamentally the concept of "rational choice" itself.

When contemporary philosophers speak of rational choice, typically they are referring to chosen courses of action that accord with established rules of logical inference and evaluatory standards. A rational choice is not one that simply makes sense or that accords with reasonable, commonsense ways of thinking or feeling, but more narrowly one that is prescribed by particular formal principles of deduction and induction. An essential condition of a decision being deemed rational is that the thinking — or, more precisely, the reasoning — behind it conform to standards that are general in nature. "We must be able," as Prado writes, "to see how potential suicidists' reasoning progresses discursively and would work for anyone in the same circumstances."[39] A rational choice must be unclouded by emotion, personal idiosyncrasy, or individual judgment. Ideally, a good computer ought to be able to follow its logic. While it is not the course of action we would always take, it remains the action we ought to take or that we would take were we fully rational.

So conceived, rational choice has its home in the domain of economics (although even many economists would dispute this), and is closely affiliated with such academic disciplines as philosophical logic and computational science. Yet whether this eminently formal, even mechanistic, conception of reason is transferable to the realm of profound life decisions of the kind we are discussing is doubtful in the extreme. When the choice before one is life or death — a choice confronted not in a classroom or on an accountant's ledger, but in the most intimate recesses of the self, and typically in the midst of profound suffering — one is not concerned about whether the option one is contemplating conforms to formal principles of rationality. Nor ought one to be so concerned. Indeed, were one's decision on such an issue to depend even in part on the outcome of a logical calculus of this or any sort, I would venture to say that such a decision would be less "rational" or philosophical than pathological.

Here we are speaking of an issue appropriately described as existential. It is, after all, nothing less than our very being that is at stake — who we are, what the ultimate significance of our existence has been, and whether our continued existence would continue to hold meaning for us. It is an issue that is radically particular to the circumstances and character of the individual in question. The thinking that culminates in a decision is unlikely to be generalizable in the sense that it could be expected to apply more or less automatically to other persons facing similar circumstances. It is the nature of existential decisions to be so particular, context specific, and personal as to be almost necessarily beyond generalized application. They are by nature passionate decisions that engage not only the rational faculty but the whole being of the individual chooser. They are also by nature free decisions, questions for which there are no true or false, correct or incorrect, or otherwise authoritative answers. As Jean-Paul Sartre would say, there are no criteria by which to decide, yet one must decide.

We cannot understand, much less assess the rationality of, suicidal acts, so to speak, from the outside in. Like any issue, suicide must be approached from an appropriate standpoint and with an appropriate set of questions in view. That standpoint is not that of the disinterested spectator or juror pronouncing observations and moral verdicts from the sidelines. Still less is it that of the Monday morning quarterback who inspects the logic of the suicidal act after the fact while unable or uninterested in saying anything of significance in the moment of decision. To understand suicide we must do so from the inside out, or from the standpoint of the individual experiencer. The rest is inconsequential.

The question whether elective death ever conforms to rules of correct reasoning is quite simply irrelevant. We do not confront death as calculating intellects, nor do we make existential choices in the fashion that we purchase consumer goods — scrupulously tallying our costs and benefits — but out of the passionate inner depths of our being.

35

Suicide and moral duty. Whatever else suicide is — an act of despair, desperation, madness, or freedom — it is not a violation of moral duty. This much may be stated categorically. All arguments in favor of the traditional suicide taboo stand or fall on the assumption that elective death is either a product of mental illness or an unethical act, and frequently both. The assumption of mental illness I shall discuss at a later point. For now, I should like to pose the question whether there is anything unethical about the suicidal act, any violation of duty or principle that it commits.

As mentioned, the traditional Christian assumption has it that the timing of one's death is in no case an issue of personal choice for the reason that such a choice infringes on a domain rightfully belonging to the Creator. In a sense, one's life is not something over which one possesses ultimate jurisdiction. This belief does not translate well into modern, secular language, yet it has remained largely presupposed in popular morality and often in moral philosophy as well that there is something fundamentally unethical about suicide, some moral taint which justifies disapproval of the act or even of persons close to the suicidal individual. Without the assumption that one's life is not one's own, however, the conclusion that suicide is immoral does not stand.

For many, it is but a short step from "I value . . ." to "you should . . ." Most of us hold the conviction that life possesses infinite value, so much so that even to ask the question, exactly how valuable life is, is greeted with something akin to indignation. Surely, we feel, one should know that human existence bears a value that is beyond price, self-evident, and absolute. Anyone who would ask about its value must either be joking, mad, or immoral. Yet immoral is precisely what it is not. The commitment most of us have toward life is never a consequence of moral obligation. The words "you should value life" have, I suspect, never persuaded a soul who had been in doubt about the matter. We value life — specifically one's own life — not out of moral duty but as a spontaneous affirmation arising on the basis of a successful or joyous experience of living, an experience of growth and maturation, of overcoming obstacles and expending energies toward a creative purpose. We embrace life when life itself, as it were, works through us, emerging spontaneously through physical action and sensation, emotional connection and creative expression. Yet no sooner do we experience the value of life than we transform it into an obligation, judging that all others must do the same, and that they are positively indecent if they do not. It is a similar phenomenon to the religious neophyte who, upon being "enlightened" or "born again," proceeds to insist that all others follow suit, and condemns those who do not.

A life experienced as joyful and infinitely worthwhile is something many are virtually born into, while others must struggle for it every day of their lives. The second group is more likely than the first to perceive the contingency of the value that human life holds. Those who have never perceived such contingencies are easily tempted into the view that those who do are morally deficient, when in fact they are anything but. Having struggled to make their lives something of value, and having glimpsed the alternative, they are if anything better situated than the first group to remark upon the value of human existence and our alleged obligation to continue it under all possible circumstances. In this group, I suspect, one would find few absolutists, but rather an appreciation of the contingencies of life or even of the will to live itself.

Human life is many things: a struggle, a journey, an adventure, a process, yet a duty it is not. One's personal existence is more akin to a choice, or series of choices, than something one is ever morally obliged to continue. If the belief that our lives are the property of a divine being carries less influence than in former times, still the idea persists that the suicidal individual is "selfish" or commits a moral transgression in electing no longer to continue, for the sake of other persons, an existence that has become disagreeable. On this view, one's right to choose matters less than other persons' estimations of the value of one's life, a view that gets the matter backwards. There is no decision more profoundly personal, and more rightfully one's own, than the choice of life or death. We may all take the view that the life of the suicidal individual is eminently valuable and meaningful, but unless the individual in question shares our view, it is irrelevant. It is not the value of life from our point of view that matters, but their personal estimation of its meaning and their right to choose in this light.

So much confusion has surrounded this issue, and for so long, that we remain uncomfortable with the knowledge that our lives are indeed our own, and with the implications of that knowledge. One implication is that the choice between life and death belongs no more to public opinion or to persons close to the suicidal individual than to an unseen power, but to the individual alone.

36

The meaning of suicide. Opinions regarding the meaning or fundamental significance of the suicidal act have included, in the main, suicide as sin, as crime, as an act of ultimate selfishness, and as a product of mental disorder. In each instance suicide is approached from the outside in, as well as from a standpoint of purported authority, be it moral, religious, legal, or scientific. I have suggested that for the issue to be understood in an appropriate light it must be comprehended as an existential decision, which means that the only relevant interpretive standpoint is that of the suicidal individual in the moment of decision. Ultimately, the issue of suicide is neither a question of rationality, morality, law, religion, nor even sociology or psychology. It is a question of existential meaning. As such, it is not a question for which we would expect to find a single "true" or authoritative answer.

There are many instances in which suicide may indeed be described in unflattering terms as an act of insanity or desperation, as a failure to realize a potential or to overcome a misfortune it was within their means to overcome. But there are many other instances in which it is not a shortcoming or failing of any kind. From the point of view of the experiencer, elective death may be an act of freedom and self-respect, of protest and rebellion, of relief from suffering, of honor, glory, or even reunion with a deceased person.

Were we to consider all suicidal acts that have been committed or attempted in all times and places, it would become evident immediately how many meanings are attributable to the act we are discussing. For the soldier embarked on a suicide mission in wartime, it is an act of ultimate commitment to a mission in which he deeply believes. For a terminally ill patient undergoing unendurable suffering, it is a final release and liberation from a condition without meaning and beyond one's control. In Japanese history it has been (or has been presented as) a means of overcoming shame, or indeed of personal and familial vindication in the face of shame. For a Buddhist monk during the Vietnam War, it was an act of political protest. For the grief-stricken, it is a form of reunion (real or imagined) with a deceased person without whom one does not care to live. For the aging person facing certain decline into incapacity, it is an act of respect for the person one has been and can no longer be.

It comes as no surprise that this most private act should bear more than a single meaning, but is contingent on the character of individuals and the particular circumstances in which they find themselves. Suicide is neither to be prescribed nor proscribed in general terms, but comprehended in its concrete specificity.

37

The choice to live. Even were we to grant the absolutist's premise — that human life is sacrosanct, always and everywhere — does
the conclusion necessarily follow that life must never be a choice,
that we must never think about it except perhaps to congratulate
ourselves on the path we have followed (but not chosen)? What
strangeness is it to believe, as traditionally we have, that the more
important a given course of action or belief is, the less it ought to be
a matter for personal choice? This is an ancient assumption, and one
that is no less widespread at present than at any previous time in
history. Specifically, the assumption states that once the truth has
been won, there is no longer any need for liberty; since liberty can
lead only in two directions — either back to the truth (where we
were in the first place, and might just as well never have left) or into
falsehood, madness, and the devil — liberty serves no purpose but
to facilitate error. Were it the case that the quest for truth, when
successful, entails the abandonment of human freedom, I should become an apostle of falsehood.

Life suffers no indignity or loss of value in becoming an object
of choice. On the contrary, the explicit choice to continue living
may invest a life with a value and meaning greater than it previously
had. It may recommit us to the path we have followed, making it
not only the "correct" path (in the eyes of the absolutist) but the
path that is one's own. This holds for each of the more profound
commitments that we make in the course of living. A commitment
between romantic partners is not lessened but deepened in being
rechosen occasionally. To reaffirm is not only to recall a previous
choice, but to rechoose it where more than a single option exists.
One does not choose in the absence of genuine alternatives.

38

Preemptive suicide. Making our lives our own — transforming them from mere existence into objects of self-chosen meaning — is among the more imperative tasks of being human. Part of that task may include making our deaths our own, such that death is no longer merely the end of a life, but in a sense its culmination. This is not always a possibility, of course. Sudden or accidental death may remove it entirely. But when there is time to contemplate death as an approaching certainty, one may choose to die as one has lived, and as the person one has been.

How difficult is it for us to imagine the position of someone who, confronted with the certainty of impending deterioration into incompetence, elects to die before such deterioration sets in, or perhaps before it reaches a point at which one is no longer the person one was? Is it inconceivable that such a person would choose to preempt such a development by means of voluntary death while in perfect awareness of the choice he or she is making? It is often maintained that suicide could never be a sane choice, yet where, precisely, is the insanity in choosing the timing of our deaths when its indefinite postponement is no longer possible, or when the only prospect that life holds for us is a condition in which we may no longer be ourselves? Not all battles are worth fighting, or fighting beyond the point at which hopelessness is not a symptom of mental illness but real. Moreover, the will to fight is not always present, and its absence is not necessarily a failing. Nonetheless, we typically admire those who fight to the end, almost regardless of the battle they are waging. We admire the courage and determination of those who bear their cross to the end, while often taking an ambivalent, even hostile, attitude toward any who do not see the value of doing so.

Preemptive suicide, when committed in full consciousness of one's prognosis and alternatives, may be less an act of "giving up" than of self-respect and self-definition. It may be one final act of freedom within a condition of unfreedom — of meaningless suffering and cold institutionalization. Such an act may transform a mere event — the cessation of biological life — into an object of meaning. Such a possibility is effectively denied by those who support the option of elective death only when a patient is experiencing extreme suffering and death would be imminent in any event. Here, suicide is considered a viable choice only when it is not a choice at all, but is coerced by circumstances beyond anyone's control and the power of medical technology. This idea, frequently encountered among defenders of the right to die, illustrates the conviction (as ancient as it is heartfelt) that our lives are not our own. It is often in the midst of suffering that we are reminded of the contingency of the will to live, but it is not only when suffering is overwhelmingly present that this is the case or that elective death is morally permissible.

39

Assisted suicide. If life is never a duty but a choice, then there is nothing inherently unethical about the suicidal act. When someone close to us chooses death over life, we may be profoundly anguished, shocked, and bewildered, but we have no cause for indignation. We may question the wisdom of their choice, but not their right to make it (on the assumption that they are mentally competent adults).

Advances in medical technology have added more than a little complexity to this issue. The question of assisted suicide has become rather pressing in recent years, compelling legislators and theorists to identify standards by which such assistance may be provided. While in most Western nations assisted suicide continues to be illegal, increasing popular acceptance of the practice combined with right-to-die activism make it probable that assisted suicide will eventually be decriminalized. It is, as well, a practice that many medical professionals have long been performing, unspoken, upon patients in the final stages of terminal illness. The question facing us is whether physicians and nurses may rightfully assist suicidal individuals who are without the means of carrying out the act, including persons who are irreversibly comatose and therefore unable to choose.

Convention has it, of course, that they may not. Since, according to tradition, suicide is immoral, providing assistance to the suicidal individual must also be immoral, as well as criminal. Yet if the choice of life or death is, as I have described it, an existential choice unencumbered by moral obligations, what does this entail in cases where the individual is able to choose but is unable to act, or is even unable to choose due to irreversible unconsciousness? By far the most frequently heard reply is that "it is a difficult issue." This is true, of course (if somewhat un-illuminating), yet in another sense perhaps the difficulty has been slightly overstated.

Psychologically, it is far from easy for medical professionals trained in the art of healing to take on the role of which we are speaking. It is perfectly understandable that physicians often protest or refuse what they perceive as the role of executioner, just as relatives are often more than slightly uneasy with the choice to discontinue treatment of someone close to them, even while knowing that it is, or would be, the wish of the individual in question. But while the psychological or emotional difficulty of making such decisions cannot be overstated, the moral difficulty can. In the case of a mentally competent adult requesting assistance in the commission of suicide from a physician, that physician violates no principle of morality in granting such assistance. While the physician is not morally obligated to grant it, and may therefore rightfully refuse for any reason, it is altogether appropriate to assist such a patient under certain conditions.

We must be very careful in setting down these conditions, of course, yet the premise on which they are based is relatively straightforward: it is up to the patient to decide his or her fate. It is neither the physician, the medical profession, conventional morality, nor even close relatives who hold the right and responsibility of deciding the fate of the patient, but the patient alone. The first condition, then, of assisted suicide is that the patient must express unambiguously and repeatedly a sincere wish to die. While some wavering on the issue is to be expected, the decision must be resolute and represent the individual's final word on the subject. Second, since it is informed choices alone that matter, the patient must be informed of his or her prognosis, the probability of recovery or remission, and so on, to the full extent of the physician's knowledge. Third, the patient must be mentally competent, meaning that he or she is an adult and is not suffering from mental illness (which does not include the grief that is natural for persons facing death).

Some theorists undoubtedly would insist that such criteria be spelled out in greater detail. I shall resist doing so, however, for the reason that flexibility is imperative for an issue in which particular cases vary dramatically and cannot always be anticipated in advance. Intelligent application of these or any ethical standards requires practical judgment rather than explicit rules governing all possible eventualities.

In the circumstance that a patient close to death becomes irreversibly comatose, and is therefore unable to decide whether to exhaust all avenues of treatment to the limits of medical technology or to be allowed to die, the overriding consideration becomes what the patient would have chosen, as best as that can be determined. The matter is relatively straightforward in cases where the patient has created an advance directive detailing his or her wishes in light of various medical eventualities. Living wills and do-not -resuscitate orders, for instance, clarify a person's wishes in the event of situations of this kind. In the absence of such documents, it falls to relatives or others close to the patient to decide what the latter would likely have wished, given the patient's values and character. Since we cannot read the patient's mind, this is an uncertain undertaking, yet in the large majority of cases determining what the patient would likely have wanted is not extraordinarily difficult for persons close to him or her. Here again, the moral premise is that the wishes of the patient are paramount in determining the course of action to be taken, whether the patient is able to participate directly and consciously in the decision-making process or not.

40

Paternalism and intervention. Is it always the case, then, that the wishes of the suicidal individual must go uncontested, or is intervention sometimes the appropriate course? Very often, as we know, persons contemplating self-destruction are either not yet adults, are suffering from depression or another psychological affliction, or are overcome by a fleeting impulse. They may radically misperceive the circumstances they are in, or underestimate the options available to them which may alleviate those circumstances. Or they may simply give up a battle that is within their means to win, but which they choose — wisely or unwisely — no longer to take up. In what circumstances are we justified in intervening when intervention goes beyond well-intentioned advice to forcible restraint, in particular legal restraint?

This being an ethical question, we get a handle on the matter by identifying the principle on which the question properly turns. That principle, I would suggest, is identical to that invoked above in approaching issues of assisted and preemptive suicide: the freedom of the individual to decide his or her fate. On the face of it, this premise appears to rule out categorically all forms of intervention or paternalism beyond simple advice; however, it is a mistake to regard human freedom as something that is maximized simply by leaving the individual alone. We are free when we possess, among other things, the competence, knowledge, and options that together make free choice possible, and not simply when our actions are unimpeded by others. A depressed adolescent's freedom is not maximized in being left alone to commit suicide.

The rationale for intervention in such a case — including intervention by the state — is that such an individual has yet to attain fully the capacity to make free decisions, particularly decisions that affect (or destroy altogether) one's future capacity to choose. It is for the sake of the adolescent's future autonomy, rather than our opinion as to what constitutes his well-being, that his present options are justifiably limited. If the suicidal wish persists until maturity and is not a product of mental illness, the moral justification of intervention is no longer present.

Forcible intervention, then, is not legitimized on the grounds that it is in the interests of the society to intervene, or that continued life is in the "real interests" of the suicidal individual, still less that the individual is not within his or her rights in choosing death over life. Nor even is it an accurate description of intervention to say that we are limiting individual freedom for that person's own good. In intervening, we are safeguarding that individual's own freedom from that which threatens it — most often mental illness or another form of incapacity.

41

Suicide and mental illness. A common reply to the above has it that suicidal persons are always suffering from mental illness, most often depression. Sane people do not commit suicide under any circumstances, this view categorically states. Those who do are not exercising their freedom but, on the contrary, succumbing to forces over which they have no, or little, control. Such forces, be they psychological or "social," therefore have the status of "causes." The choice between life and death, in this frequently encountered view, is in no case an existential decision but is a medical problem or a product of environmental or psychological causes.

This view was classically presented, albeit in different forms, by Emile Durkheim and Sigmund Freud. While Freud introduced the theory of the death instinct, or "Thanatos," to account for suicide, world war, and other phenomena relating to death, Durkheim in his monumental study of suicide popularized the interpretation of this act as a product of social causes from which the individual is essentially unfree. Social reality, Durkheim asserted, maintains a firm grip upon the individual, so much so that the phenomenon of suicide is properly understood not from the standpoint of suicidal persons and the meaning which that act holds for them, but from the standpoint of societies and the social causes that compel individuals toward self-destruction. Indeed, for Durkheim and many sociologists and "suicidologists" after him, suicide is "in itself a collective phenomenon,"[40] something to be studied less as a phenomenon of individual psychology than as a phenomenon of the group. As such, it naturally lends itself to sociological investigation, using scientific tools of analysis like statistical comparison, analysis of demographic norms and socio-economic indicators, and so on. Above all, it is the comparison of suicide rates within and between populations that reveals the true causes of suicide, Durkheim and many others following him maintain.

Among the conclusions Durkheim reached regarding the causes of suicide are the following: "Suicide varies inversely with the degree of integration of religious society. Suicide varies inversely with the degree of integration of domestic society. Suicide varies inversely with the degree of integration of political society."[41] The disintegration of each of these elements of modern life, Durkheim asserted, has caused a general increase in suicide rates. The phenomenon of "egoistic suicide" in particular is brought on by "excessive individuation"[42] from the mass. Its sole remedy, in his words, "is to restore enough consistency to social groups for them to obtain a firmer grip on the individual, and for him to feel himself bound to them."[43] Durkheim expressed much the same point elsewhere: "First of all, it can be said that, as collective force is one of the obstacles best calculated to restrain suicide, its weakening involves a development of suicide. When society is strongly integrated, it holds individuals under its control, considers them at its service and thus forbids them to dispose willfully of themselves. Accordingly, it opposes their evading their duties to it through death."[44] The ominous implications of Durkheim's remarks regarding the relationship between the individual and the social whole are unmistakable. Since the individual is essentially a social product, "we" (the social whole, including the state) are well within our rights in engineering individuality and individual behavior as we think best. We need not worry about personal freedom since such freedom is largely illusory, and what passes for it produces social disintegration and an escalated suicide rate.

Ultimately, Durkheim's theory of suicide is less scientific than political and moral. Its conclusion is that it is the business of social and political institutions to "manage" individuality according to the requirements of collective well-being while optimizing conformity ("integration"). The language of science is used to advance a political agenda, as so often happens when sociologists seek to remedy the social ills that they describe.

So much confusion surrounds the issue of suicide that it is far from clear exactly what kind of issue we are discussing. Suicide is essentially neither a political problem nor a social ill. With the exception of the question of intervention, it is not the business of "society" at all, but is a profoundly personal, existential issue. As such, it calls for respectful distance rather than anxious fretting and institutional management. Framing the issue in this way means challenging the assumption that suicide is invariably pathological or a product of causes compelling individuals toward self-destruction. As sociologists and psychologists themselves increasingly recognize, it is a myth that only the mentally ill commit suicide. Persons who voluntarily end their lives (including the large number of those who do so sub-intentionally) may perceive their circumstances with perfect clarity. The hopelessness they feel may reflect precisely the reality of their situations. We may witness the deliberation behind the decision and conclude that it is not symptomatic of depression or delusional thinking, but eminently understandable under the circumstances. Neither are suicidal persons necessarily succumbing to social forces beyond their understanding or control, but may be acting on a decision that is entirely voluntary.

General statements regarding an issue as complex as this one are difficult to prove, and the burden of proof falls on those who defend the hypothesis that suicide in general is a product either of mental illness or of social causes. What if the "cause" of suicide in a given case is simply existential distress, an absence of meaning in one's life, or in the only kind of life that is possible for one facing incapacity or extreme suffering? What sort of "cause" is this? Indeed, it is not a cause at all, but a choice bearing upon a personal estimation of how worthwhile a life is — in particular, one's own life under a given (and perhaps unchangeable) set of circumstances.

We do not understand suicide, or death in general, from the outside in, as Durkheim and many others following him have attempted to do. It is a profoundly personal phenomenon that takes us into the innermost regions of the self. Accordingly, we shall not comprehend suicide by dwelling in the region of abstract generalities and statistics, theoretical postulates and scientific proofs. The point is not to explain its alleged causes but to understand the meaning of the act — which means the meanings of it — from the standpoint of the individual agent. Suicide is often an act of desperation and despair, but it is also an act of freedom and dignity. It is tragic and it is noble, it is rebellious and impulsive, a political statement, an act of honor and glory, and sometimes (not always) a product of psychological disturbance.

42

"*A collective phenomenon.*" One thing that suicide is not is "a collective phenomenon," as Durkheim described it. We shall continue to misunderstand this act for as long as we treat it as an object of quasi-scientific investigation, putting it under a microscope, as it were, rather than interpreting its existential importance and meaning to the persons contemplating it. From a distance we may wish to describe suicide in abstract and collective terms, but we do not face death as members of a collective unit, including the abstraction that is "society." Only individual persons face death.

We face it, moreover, neither as hapless environmental products nor as doctors, lawyers, or scientists, but as human beings alone. The encounter with death is radically individualizing and brings into focus the limits of our sociability. It is somewhat of an exaggeration to say that we die as we are born — radically alone — since in facing death we continue to understand its significance in terms appropriated from our culture; when possible, we face it as well in the company of persons close to us. Yet we do not face death as bearers of social roles — roles that, however important to us in the course of living, go out the window in the confrontation with personal mortality.

43

A death instinct? In Freud's later years, he proposed the hypothesis of a death instinct ("Thanatos") which wars eternally with the instinct of life ("Eros"). It is the death instinct universally present in human psychology that explains such phenomena as suicide, war, and general destruction in human life. Many of our internal conflicts, Freud maintained, are products of a fundamental tension between the instincts of life and sexuality on one hand and a return to an actionless, pre-organic state on the other. It is a hypothesis that found few defenders, and for many (good) reasons which I shall not discuss here.

While I would not wish to defend Freud's theory of a death instinct, there is at least some intuitive plausibility in the notion of a deep-seated drive toward, if not self-destruction, then perhaps something short of this. Much of human psychology involves a vacillation between competing drives, just as our existential condition itself impels us back and forth between seeming opposites. Being human involves negotiating conflicting imperatives toward expansive vitality and contractive lethargy, motion and rest, consciousness and unconsciousness, understanding and illusion, and a thousand lesser polarities. If life itself impels us toward motion, some other drive impels us toward lethargy, standing still, or even self-destruction. Lethargy has a momentum all its own, one that surpasses the purely physiological need for rest to incorporate many of our ways of living and thinking. If we were to express the matter in the psychoanalytic language of instinctual drives, then perhaps we could posit a lethargy instinct rather than a death instinct — although the vocabulary of instincts, in my view, adds little to our understanding of the human situation. I would sooner speak in this connection of inward and existential imperatives rather than instincts, imperatives leading us to and fro between what, on the face of it at least, look like opposite pairings.

Suicide may be one manner by which such tensions are resolved. In the case of mentally competent adults, elective death is not instinctually or environmentally determined but is a way of coming to meaningful terms with one's circumstances or existential condition in general. Like any act, it may be wise or unwise, noble or tragic, but it is an act in which one's life is taken decisively into one's hands.

CHAPTER 4

THE ENCOUNTER WITH LIFE

44

Grieving and living. How we comport ourselves in the face of death is generally indicative of how we experience life itself — honestly or dishonestly, with maturity or without it. Confronting one's personal mortality and grieving the loss of another can either be carried out as tasks that engage fully our capacities of introspection, understanding, sympathy, and choice, or they can be evaded as so much unpleasantness. In death there is nothing that is remotely pleasant, yet the inclination to look honestly into the dark side of human existence is not simply a morose pastime, but is an education in the meaning and purpose of that existence.

Psychologists say that to grieve properly we must emote completely, rather than repress the painful and conflicting emotions connected with grieving; is it any less true that we must understand completely (rather than lie about) the significance of death, the extent and importance of our loss, the lessons imparted by the life of the deceased, and the extent of our freedom to choose life or death in the face of suffering? If all of this is "grief work," might there be a corresponding task implicit to living, or to living well? Perhaps grief work is not an isolated phenomenon at all, but is a concentrated version of our common life task of understanding, feeling, and choosing a manner of living with conscious will and purpose. While our everyday preoccupations and "the ways of the world" are quick to distract us from this more fundamental task of living, the encounter with death brings us back radically to this task and to ourselves.

If death educates, it does so not by imparting information to us in our bereavement, but by changing our focus. It extends our range of vision from the self-imposed narrowness of daily life to a broader and deeper perspective on life as a totality. It calls to our attention both the darker and lighter sides of human existence, and compels us to re-examine ourselves and the lives we have chosen to lead. To contemplate death with maturity and intellectual honesty is to work through the grieving process, to comprehend the meaning of a life that is now at an end, to learn the lessons which that life teaches, and to re-examine our choices in that light.

Death may be an educator, but we are not always attentive students. As any educator knows, a well-taught lesson is not always well learned. Indeed, we may choose not to grieve at all, but to distract ourselves all the more. Whether out of indifference to the deceased or simple immaturity, we may narrow our gaze still further to the minor details of life, as the student may doodle in a notebook or send notes back and forth to other students. The encounter with death can often bring out what is best in us, refocusing and recommitting us to the life that we have chosen, but so also can it bring out the worst. Above all, it brings out what is there in our character, as if the encounter with death were shone a spotlight on our interiors and our manner of living.

When we confront death in an intellectually honest fashion and refuse the distractions and evasions with which our culture is quick to provide us, what we see is that death is a sobering inevitability, and — to our knowledge — is no blessing of the kind long asserted by religion. Those who allege the certainty of an afterlife — that death is therefore not as bad as it seems — simply ignore the limits of what we can know in order to offer a palliative to the grieving or dying.

If contemplating death in an honest fashion enables us the better to understand life, as I have asserted, then what is it that death teaches about our manner of living? What is it with which we have "lost touch," as Dostoyevsky prophetically remarked?

45

Digesting experience. Among the reasons we often turn our backs on life is that life itself makes demands of us which are often simpler to ignore than to heed. Understanding the exact nature of these demands is anything but straightforward, yet to live is to be called upon to heed imperatives of certain kinds. These are demands that we are free to accept or reject, but we reject them at a price. Human beings are free agents whose "nature" is remarkably unfixed, yet existing as a human being is not without conditions and imperatives which we all sense, however dimly.

Among these is the imperative to digest our experiences. From major life events and turning points to our various successes and failures, traumatic experiences, or the ordinary events of everyday life, we work through our experiences on the analogy of digestion. This is an observation that Nietzsche brought to our attention, and which Freud and later psychoanalysts carried further. Nietzsche commented that "good digestion" is imperative to a life well lived — an observation that applies no more to diet than to the general course of experience. The grieving process provides an excellent example of this, but it is only one instance of a generally observable phenomenon. Grief is a task and a process that must be worked through in order that something resembling peaceful resolution may be possible. It is contrasted with evasion or repression in the respect that grieving requires an often slow and deliberate effort to absorb, emotionally and cognitively, what has taken place. It calls on us to come to terms with reality directly and honestly, without indulging the impulse to avoid or minimize the significance of unpleasant facts. Truth does not always set us free, but its active avoidance never does so.

The utter unpleasantness of everything connected with death gives rise to a powerful temptation to turn away from it by any means, yet the price we pay for doing so is alienation from our lives and ourselves. It creates a kind of "indigestion" that prevents us from having done with an experience which is of more than passing importance. We can do much the same with any experience; we often do in the case of any matter that is unpleasant to contemplate. In the interest of putting the mind at ease, we may refuse to contemplate an experience that caused suffering, or would cause suffering if we were to pause and reflect upon it. We choose ease and comfort at the price of failing to notice — and thereby failing to digest — what has happened to us. The experience remains with us, undigested and uncontemplated, and as a consequence is not placed into our past. Remaining with us, the experience develops a power over us, as psychoanalysts and other observers have often described. Tillich, for example, has written: "It has been rightly said that the strength of a person's character is dependent on the quantity of things that he has thrown into the past. In spite of the power his past holds over him, a man can separate himself from it, throw it out of the present into the past in which it is condemned to remain ineffective — at least for a time. It may return and conquer the present and destroy the person, but this is not necessarily so. We are not inescapably victims of our past. We can make the past remain nothing but *past*. The act in which we do this has been called 'repentance.' Genuine repentance is not the feeling of sorrow about wrong actions, but it is the act of the whole person in which he separates himself from certain elements of his being, discarding them into the past as something that no longer has any power over the present."[45]

In less religious terms, experiences exercise a certain power over us until we place them decisively into the past. We have done with an experience, particularly a painful one, by contemplating it, understanding its significance, feeling our way through it, deciding what if anything is to be done concerning it. "Repentance" and grieving are both examples of how we do this, yet they are far from unique in this respect. Any experience that is of significance to us must be digested cognitively and emotionally in order to live fully in the present and, in a sense, to be present in our actions.

Outwardly, we are always living in the present, but inwardly this is far from the case. How many of us spend years or decades of our lives unconsciously reliving the past or, less commonly, living for the future, is impossible to determine with certainty, but it is likely a higher number than we imagine. Even if we do not entirely live in the past, our refusal to have done with it keeps us there against our will, preventing us from living in the present. We are compelled to repeat old patterns again and again until we either make it right or achieve some sort of resolution. In this there is no choice: we must go back and relive the experience until it is satisfactorily worked through. How we accomplish this is a matter of choice, but the choice to leave this task unfinished compels us to relive and to repeat, often in profoundly disturbing ways.

It is, I suspect, one of the psychological functions of dreaming to work through and to interpret the events of the day in the metaphorical language of the unconscious. The recurring dream of a traumatic experience in one's past, for instance, is a re-experiencing of the original event; yet it comes not out of any simple masochistic urge, but in order that we may digest the experience to the end: to accept the reality of what has been, to experience fully its emotional impact, and to comprehend its meaning and psychological importance. One does not move beyond the experience or consign it to the past without understanding it and coming to terms with it by this means. Human beings live by our awareness and work through our experiences by bringing them to awareness, making them objects of conscious understanding and emotion. It involves more than the mere "ventilation of feelings," but the choice to attend to the events of our lives and to put them into our past in order to exist in the present.

46

The invention of meaning. It is a common saying that we cannot change the past. The past is over and done with, an object behind us which we can accept or deny, but not change. This is only half true. The events that have happened to us cannot unhappen, it is true, but the meaning of those events can and does change according to our interpretation. We decide what meaning those events will have for us; their significance is neither fixed, unchanging, nor carved into the fabric of the universe. Meaning is invariably "for us" in the sense that when we ask what the meaning of a given experience is, we are asking what it meant to us: what impact it had on our lives, how it affected our actions and choices, what we were able to learn from it, and so on. A meaningless occurrence is precisely one from which nothing followed, an isolated happening that changed us not at all.

Digesting an experience includes the act of deciding the meaning that it will hold for us, a decision that can be modified at a future time. This is a meaning that is less discovered than invented. It is imposed by an act of interpretation which takes the experience out of its isolation as a singular occurrence and places it within a larger, more comprehensive perspective. It locates that experience, for instance, in a narrative unfolding over time, transforming it from a brute fact into an episode in a continuing story in which we are the principal character. Human beings are creatures of meaning and understanding, searching every day of our lives for the significance, large or small, of what we see. Frankl speaks in this connection of a "will to meaning" as the primary source of motivation in human life:

"This meaning is unique and specific in that it must and can be fulfilled by him alone; only then does it achieve a significance which will satisfy his own *will* to meaning. There are some authors who contend that meanings and values are 'nothing but defense mechanisms, reaction formations and sublimations.' But as for myself, I would not be willing to live merely for the sake of my 'defense mechanisms,' nor would I be ready to die merely for the sake of my 'reaction formations.' Man, however, is able to live and even to die for the sake of his ideals and values!"[46]

That we are beings for whom meaning is not a luxury but a necessity has been observed as well by existential philosophers. As these writers have often observed, human beings are sustained by meanings, and live in a world (a "lifeworld") of meaningful relations and practices of various kinds. Ortega y Gasset, for example, speaks of being human as "a living problem" since the possibility of meaninglessness — of ceasing to be that which we have chosen to be, or indeed of having our very humanity taken from us — is ever-present: "[M]an lives in perpetual danger of being dehumanized. With him, not only is it problematic and contingent whether this or that will happen to him . . . but at times what happens to man is nothing less than *ceasing to be man*. And this is true not only abstractly and generically but it holds of our own individuality. Each one of us is always in danger of not being the unique and untransferable *self* which he is."[47] Heidegger too has spoken of the human being as always an issue for himself or herself, of anxiety as belonging essentially to the human condition, and of authenticity as a search for personal and self-chosen meaning. Each of us must contend with our own being, deciding how — also whether — we shall be and what the purpose of our existence will be.

It is no contradiction to suppose that meaning both sustains us and is self-chosen. It is an ancient prejudice that the ultimate significance of life must be derived from something beyond life, an otherworldly order that sustains us and provides a moral center from which to live. Another prejudice of old has it that the meaning of one's personal existence must be that of one's tradition or collective grouping. In either case, the idea is that the meaning that orients and sustains us must also transcend us, and in particular it must not be subject to personal choice. Anything that is genuinely self-chosen, in this view, is incapable of reaching into the depths of our being and sustaining us through life. Yet nothing whatsoever supports this view. The highest purposes that orient and sustain our existence need not be anything apart from the process of living itself and the values and tasks that comprise it. Life itself sustains us while being, in a sense, self-chosen; we do not choose, it is true, to enter into life, but we most certainly are free to continue or discontinue that life, or to modify our way of life. Frankl has observed at first hand how survivors of prisoner-of-war and concentration camps are able to sustain themselves through the most abject dehumanization by choosing and focusing on a task that awaits them upon liberation, including when the prospect of liberation appears dim. As Frankl recounts from his own experience in a Nazi concentration camp: "As for myself, when I was taken to the concentration camp of Auschwitz, a manuscript of mine ready for publication was confiscated. Certainly, my deep desire to write this manuscript anew helped me to survive the rigors of the camps I was in. For instance, when in a camp in Bavaria I fell ill with typhus fever, I jotted down on little scraps of paper many notes intended to enable me to rewrite the manuscript, should I live to the day of liberation. I am sure that this reconstruction of my lost manuscript in the dark barracks of a Bavarian concentration camp assisted me in overcoming the danger of cardiovascular collapse."[48] As this case eloquently illustrates, one's highest purpose or reason for living need not be generalizable to all persons, but may be entirely specific to the individual. It may be self-chosen while capable of sustaining us through the most difficult trials, as well as through the general course of living.

Among the imperatives of human existence is precisely this identification or invention of meaning, a meaning that may be shared or may be specific to one's own circumstances, but which must be authentically self-chosen in order that one's life may properly be one's own. It is through conscious participation in meanings, whether large or small, collective or personal, that the existential vacuum is replaced with a motivation and an identity that bears us through life.

47

Life and freedom. Among the principal conditions and imperatives of existing as a human being is free agency. To be human is to be without a nature that is fixed or timeless, but rather to choose who and how we shall be. As existential philosophers have long realized, human nature is without a fixed "essence," but is an "issue" that each of us resolves for ourselves by exercising our freedom. Through our deeds and decisions, we choose who we are as well as that which we shall become. This is a project that belongs to every human being as an individual, even as we often surrender our freedom to others imagined to possess superior authority or knowledge to ourselves. The choice to surrender our freedom to others is simultaneously the choice to surrender our selves since it is a self that is in the making in every act of decision.

Human life is invariably characterized by something akin to ownership; it is "my life" or "your life" that exists concretely. A life that "belongs" to no one, that is, as it were, disembodied or free-floating, does not exist. Yet at the same time to make one's life one's own is a task and, when it is accomplished, an achievement of the first order. It is also a task at which we can fail. On the face of it, this appears to be a contradiction, yet the contradiction is more apparent than real. One makes one's life one's own by means of self-chosen values and action. One can choose not to do this by permitting others to make one's decisions for one, and at a surface level one's life continues to be one's own. Yet at a deeper level, one's existence ceases to belong to one in surrendering freedom to others. It becomes questionable whose life one is leading, and who is responsible for that life.

There is, as existentialists have also realized, no one way of being human. Human existence has no blueprint of how we must be, a blueprint to which we may be expected to conform. We decide — or are capable of deciding — what our existence will be. In deciding this, we are choosing, in a sense, a type of humanity, one realized in the general course of living. We become choice-making selves, or agents, in the process of fashioning autonomous decisions and "transform[ing]," as Nietzsche writes, "every 'It was' into an 'I wanted it thus!'"[49]

To assert that human beings are the sum of their decisions and actions is not to deny the reality of genuine necessity. Undoubtedly, there are limits to human freedom, but the point I would emphasize is that it is not sheer necessity that primarily determines who or what we are, but rather how we relate to necessities. Overcoming natural necessity has long been regarded as fundamental to human existence and culture. How we comport ourselves in the face of death, physical limitation, and the "given" facts of our existence is ultimately more decisive than those facts themselves. To be human is less to be hemmed in by necessity than to struggle against it using all the capacities at our disposal, not least of which is freedom itself. The story of Sisyphus, as Camus realized, is representative of the human condition, yet not in the sense that we are condemned to a pointless fate but in that we create a type of humanity in the struggle or rebellion against what merely is or has been. We stand to our "fate" in a relationship of neither subordination nor mastery, but of unceasing tension. Life itself is a tension, or series of tensions, between what is and what might be, between nature and culture, past and future, self and others. What is "given" is not the actions we must take, but the conditions and circumstances in the midst of which we act.

Of ultimate importance is whether the stand we take in the face of these conditions and circumstances is a product of our freedom or of its surrender. If freely chosen, this stand and this life become our own. Otherwise, we surrender ourselves to other persons or to public opinion in exchange for acceptance or security. When we relinquish our freedom, we do so willingly, but usually unwittingly and in small degrees. We dispense with it in imperceptible quantities for small comforts and satisfactions of numerous kinds.

Only the accumulated result of the freedom we have surrendered becomes visible, and then only dimly. Since freedom is inseparable from responsibility, the loss of the former entails a corresponding loss of the latter. As we lose control over the forces that govern our lives, our lives not only cease to be our own, they become products of no one's choices and no one's responsibility. Given the frequency with which we sell our freedom for security, it is no surprise if we should sometimes feel that others (authorities, government, institutions) are ultimately responsible for what becomes of us.

48

Standing out. To be human is to stand to our "fate," or the unchangeable realities of our condition, in a certain fashion — one of neither submission nor mastery, but of dynamic tension. It is also to stand within a social environment. We are always inheritors of tradition, language, social roles and practices, belief systems, and a comprehensive way of life. An individual life occurs invariably within an environmental and cultural context. It is this environment that provides us with a fundamental understanding of the world, ourselves, and the values that orient our conduct.

This observation has become widely accepted, yet we easily overestimate the consequences that follow from this. Determinists, for example, pronounce that the individual is nothing but a product of his or her environment, a rather docile creature for whom freedom and dignity are passé notions. In less extreme form, many on the political left argue that because the individual is a thoroughly socialized being, political and other institutions must also be socialized. If the individual is an environmental product, the argument often goes, we might as well manipulate that environment in order to produce the kind of individuals we want. Arguments of this sort come in many forms and range in subtlety. Typically, they overlook two things.

First, as I have noted above, individuals stand to their "fate," including their environment, not as passive subjects, but in a dynamic tension. We are neither masters of our fate nor slaves to it, but something intermediate between the two. We shape our environment even as it shapes us, selecting which values and beliefs among those we inherit we shall continue to uphold, and what creative modifications to tradition or our environment we shall introduce. That we are shaped by our social environment does not preclude the possibility of resistance or rebellion against particular features of that environment. Indeed, it is a commonplace for individuals to question and modify aspects of their environment as a means of enhancing their lives and changing their corner of the world for the better (or the better by their lights).

Second, human beings not only stand within an environment, they also stand out from it. It is not as a form of narcissism or adolescent rebellion that individuals seek to distinguish themselves in one fashion or another from the mass. Much of our identity is bound up with the way in which we stand out from our social environment, even as much of it is also derived from our participation within it. Indeed, to say that each of us "participates" in a social or cultural environment is already to suggest a degree of free agency and scope for individual difference in our relationship with our environment. Our manner of participation can be more or less rebellious, more or less conformist, but in any event it does not resemble submission to something over which we have no control or from which we may not stand out.

One of the oddities of modern culture is that while we tend to admire most those who distinguish themselves through their achievements, with equal frequency we speak in negative terms of those who "protrude," who are "eccentric" or "out of step." Children especially are discouraged from being "removed" or "uncooperative," not least by educators who warn at the same time of the dangers of conformity. We lament the inability of many young people to resist "peer pressure" and conformity while having taught them from the earliest age to obey and to "get along" at virtually any price.

The ambivalence in modern culture toward standing out most likely stems from the fear of isolation or ridicule which keeps us "in step," even as we privately long for rebellion or any kind of distinction. The longing for security keeps us in step with our environment and the established order, even as the voice of life itself moves us often in the opposite direction. Mass society makes it increasingly possible to disappear into a crowd and accentuates the dangers of social isolation, partly as a means of self-legitimation while also serving the instinct of security. "Fitting in" creates safety while standing out is a source of danger and difficulty. If being human is a task, much of it is spent negotiating these conflicting imperatives. Each of us accomplishes this task in one fashion or other in the course of living, selecting occasions in which each instinct may predominate over the other. We cannot always stand out, any more than we can always conform, but as existentialists are inclined to point out, we gain a deeper connection with life and with ourselves when we consciously take upon ourselves the burden of standing out from the mass.

49

Making ourselves at home in the world. To say that human life is always played out within a social or cultural environment, and that
this environment fundamentally affects both who we are and how
we live, tells only half the story of the complex relationship between
the individual and the social world. In this relationship, individuals
are fashioned by an environment even as they endeavor to refashion
it, and conflicting imperatives of social belonging and private retreat
are negotiated by each of us in one manner or other. To this I would
add that among the complexities of existing in a social world, and of
human life itself, is the project of making ourselves at home in that
world.

It is not entirely "by nature" or automatically that we are at
home in the world. In the world of nature, human beings have long
been without the instincts that would enable us to negotiate our
way through the natural environment with the facility of other species. In the environment in which we are most at home — the world
of social relationships, culture, and tradition — we are still faced
with a task that we must carry out in the general course of living.
This is the task of overcoming alienation in its various forms, and in
so doing making ourselves at home in the world.

To illustrate this, consider the familiar experience of moving to
a new city. The original feeling of being a stranger in an alien place
is overcome by such means as finding a home and employment,
gaining familiarity with our surroundings, entering new relationships, taking up projects that engage us with others in our environment, and absorbing the general culture. In each instance, we are
transforming the foreign into the familiar, creating a fit between

ourselves and our environment such that the latter is no longer perceived as an alien domain but a place where we are at home. Moving to a different city is an accelerated form of a process in which we are continually engaged. This is a life process of overcoming alienation and finding our way about the world, adjusting to it while also transforming it (or a corner of it) to suit our own requirements. Through our actions and projects, we make ourselves at home in whatever environment we find ourselves, from the general culture to a neighborhood, workplace, or what have you.

To make oneself at home involves more than gaining information about our surroundings, finding out how things are done, and feeling at ease. It involves, more fundamentally, a process of refashioning aspects of our environment after our own image, imposing our identity or sensibilities on our surroundings without "being imposing." It involves standing out from the mass and creating meaning where there was none. At the same time, making ourselves at home in the world involves taking possession of ourselves, adapting to what surrounds us while carving out a place for ourselves which accords with who we are. Being at home in an environment crucially involves gaining an understanding of its workings, being able to negotiate our way through it, establishing a fit between it and ourselves, and seeing a part of ourselves reflected in that environment. It is neither to submit to an established order nor to dominate the scene, but to pursue an intermediate course of mutual adjustment.

50

Fashioning identity. That we are members of the biological species *homo sapiens* is a given fact of our existence. That we are inheritors of a particular culture, language, and tradition is also a given, although our manner of participation in each includes the possibility, or indeed the necessity, of freedom. That we are bearers of individual identity, however, is very far from a given or fixed reality. We gain a sense of who we are, it is true, from our involvement in a social environment, including traditional roles, practices, and values which provide us with a basic orientation to the world and a sense of our personal identity. However, it is mistaken to regard the matter of who we are as one that is fixed, absolute, or revisable only to a minor degree. The human being, as Heidegger rightly observed, is invariably an issue for himself or herself. Who we are and how we live are issues for each of us to resolve freely.

Among the ways that we encounter life, and make our lives our own, is precisely by taking upon ourselves the task of fashioning our own identity. This is not accomplished in a social vacuum, but neither is it accomplished merely by belonging to a social environment. It is accomplished over the course of a lifetime through actions, decisions, relationships, and values. It is difficult to overstate the complexity of the problem of determining who someone is, including oneself. If the self may be likened to a story unfolding over time, then the identity of that self is composed of the chapters and episodes that make up the course of the narrative. The identity of a character in a novel is defined by that character's words and deeds, as well as what others say about him or her. There is no need to suppose that who that character "really" is, is someone or something apart from what he does and says — some underlying essence that cannot be observed. The same can be said about real persons. We are the accumulated sum of our choices and experiences, thus to a large degree a product of our own freedom. In making choices, it is ourselves that we are choosing. In subscribing to a system of values and beliefs, we are identifying ourselves with a type of humanity. In realizing a potentiality, creating values, and standing out, we "become who we are," as Nietzsche would say.

This last phrase of Nietzsche's suggests that who each of us is is not something static or fixed once and for all ("being"), but something continually fashioned by the self in the process of living ("becoming"). As Nietzsche also observed, one may know a person by her "style," or by the way in which she comports herself and by the underlying unity or coherence of her habits. We "give style" to our character by arranging each of our traits and actions into an integrated whole. To do so in full self-consciousness is "a great and rare art"[50] — rare because the issue of who we are is seldom confronted directly as a task and a choice. Most often, we regard our identity as something settled and beyond choice rather than an issue that we may freely resolve. It is, we often suppose, something discovered rather than invented. That the reverse is closer to the truth may be seen if we consider the practical role that an awareness of personal identity plays in every human life.

When we commit a misdeed, we are often said to be "forgetting ourselves." This suggestive phrase implies that each of us carries about with us in the course of our lives a basic understanding of who we are, and that this self-understanding is related directly to the moral conscience. When we act unethically, it is not only our conscience we betray but our identity as well (and, of course, the person we are harming). We lose sight of, or forget, not only principles of right and wrong, but ourselves or the kind of self we are striving to become. An explicit sense of who we are — as well as of the meaning of our existence — sustains us in life. In the present day and age, to say that we are "forgetting ourselves" means that we are forgetting not our immortal soul but the commitments we have made, our habitual ways of acting, and our sense of self.

That living crucially involves an awareness of individual identity may be seen as well in contemplating a distinction often drawn between "living" and "surviving." We commonly speak of an individual as merely surviving if, for instance, that person contracts a terminal illness, loses all prospect of recovery or remission, and finally becomes irreversibly comatose. A "vegetable," we say, merely survives. Yet what indignity is it to survive only? To survive, we might say, is to fulfill the basic conditions of biological life; it is a state of the organism in which the vital organs continue their operations, yet where one is no longer the person one was. One's individual being — particularly one's awareness and self-awareness — is no longer present. In a sense, one is no longer a particular individual, but a physical body only.

Fashioning an identity and carrying it about with us as a self-conscious act are fundamental to the task of being human. It is this that enables us all the more to stand out and to experience ourselves as beings of absolute worth. Here we have a relationship of mutual reinforcement: standing out from the mass provides us with an identity that is distinctly our own, while the consciousness of that identity enables us to stand out and to affirm our individuality all the more. It is precisely this awareness of personal identity that provides the ground of the elementary experience of feeling that one has a right to exist in this world. It is among the fundamental differences between adolescence and maturity that the latter has gained a sense of selfhood that the former typically has not, and as a consequence senses fundamentally its right to be that which it is. It will not willingly subordinate itself, given what it has struggled to become, while awkward adolescence often feels itself an interloper upon the earth. Adolescence cannot resolutely assert its right to exist when it has yet to become what it is.

51

Cultivating inwardness. To the extent that modern culture directs our attention toward outward things — from material comfort and middle class respectability to conformity, external appearances, and reputation — it diverts us from our own inner depths and the task of cultivating these as a condition of a meaningful existence. When Socrates provocatively announced that "the unexamined life is not worth living," he was calling us back from the preoccupation with appearances and outward things toward a deeper, more meaningful, and also a more human connection with life. This is not unlike the turn within to which the encounter with death invites us, a call to "know thyself," to put aside the distractions of ordinary life and to re-establish a more vital connection with ourselves.

Conditions of modern life often lead us to overlook that human life is lived not only on the outside, or at a surface level, but that there are deeper, quieter ways of being alive. In addition to having things, doing things, and appearing respectable, there is also being something that is inherently worth being. There are modes of living from our inner depths which have nothing to do with mysticism or escapism of any sort. Indeed, what is escapist is precisely the outer-directedness and self-imposed unreflectiveness of modern life, conditions that provide escape from the existential vacuum which so many experience in contemporary culture. It is through the cultivation of inwardness that it becomes possible for our outward actions and relationships to take on a degree of authenticity and genuineness which, as modes of escape, they invariably lack. Being fully present and engaged in outward acts is impossible except on a basis of a meaningful interiority, or unless our actions proceed from a self with a defined identity, purpose, and capacity for inwardness.

This last point warrants some emphasis. We are so often inclined to regard the inner life as either a flight from reality or a morbid obsession that we become disconnected from ourselves while also neglecting that which makes effective outward action possible. A meaningful interiority is the necessary ground of an effective exteriority.

If cultivating inwardness is a life task belonging to each of us, by what steps do we achieve this? Or indeed is this something that may be achieved at all? Is it not simply a given fact of one's personality that one is either "introverted" or "extroverted," oriented by nature or conditioning toward the inner or outer life? Are our inner depths not also given — either we possess them in some abundance or we carry within us an emptiness, about which there is nothing to be done but perhaps to avoid dwelling on it? Here I would suggest once again that there is remarkably little about the human being that is fixed, absolute, or beyond the freedom to revise. "Human nature" is as much "second nature," hence a product of our freedom, as it is a fixed reality. We may cultivate our inner depths by any variety of means, none of which requires extended sojourns to India in order to accomplish. There is the art of quiet reflection, contemplation of our reason for living or of the person we wish to become. There is remembrance of the person we have been, understanding the influence exercised upon us by particular experiences and persons from our past. There is the explicit perception and appreciation of what surrounds us. There is the art of taking our identity into our hands and fashioning decisions resolutely on its basis. There is aesthetic appreciation, being attuned with our physicality, and exercising our capacity of emotional awareness. There is solitude and stillness, symbolized in religious terms by the retreat into the desert or the forest. Except metaphorically, one need not withdraw to the desert for forty days and forty nights in order to retreat into the self or to cultivate inwardness. This is accomplished in the ordinary course of living and by leading, at least in certain moments, what Socrates called "the examined life."

52

Investing ourselves in our actions. What is it to be "in touch with life" but to lead an "examined life" or, more broadly, to live from out of the depths of our being? Does it not involve a capacity to draw upon our inner resources and identity in performing outward actions, and to have our actions in turn confirm or reconfirm our identity as persons? Nietzsche writes: "That *your* Self be in the action, as the mother is in the child: let that be *your* maxim of virtue!"[51] In one sentence Nietzsche encapsulates not only one of the most fundamental principles of ethics, but an equally fundamental principle of life itself. To live as a human being is to live by one's consciousness and understanding, to be attuned to experiences both internal and external, and in so doing to be fully "present" in our actions.

Other species appear to do this, or something very much like it, automatically. Their modes of life require constant alertness to their environment, while their actions proceed (or, at least, appear to) directly from their "nature" or instincts. There is no question whether a predator in the wild is fully "present" in the acts of pursuing and devouring its prey; it could not be more so. Human beings, having no fixed nature or instincts sufficient to guide us through life, must do this by choice. We are attuned, cognitively and emotionally, to our environment — or not — by choice. We are present in our actions — or not — also by choice. To be present in our actions, as Nietzsche here suggests, is to "give birth" to them, or to invest our internal sense of who we are in outward form. It is to regard our actions as forms of self-expression. Artists are well acquainted with this. A work of art, if worthy of the name, is not disconnected from its creator. It is not merely a commercial enterprise, but is an act of self-expression that resonates deeply within the artist no less than the audience. The imperative to create is an imperative to express, to "give birth" to outward form as (in part, at least) a reflection of one's interiors.

Living from the depths of our being is precisely the art of investing a self-chosen identity and potentiality in our outward acts, and in turn recognizing how these acts work to refashion or reaffirm that identity. Whether we are expressly aware of it or not, our actions and decisions simultaneously express, affirm, and refashion our identity. Most often, this process unfolds without our conscious awareness; only its consequences are fully apparent to us. We feel either an elementary sense of well being and of being at home in the world, or of frustration and alienation. That these are products of our own choices is far less apparent, particularly when the world is quick to assure us that such matters are quite beyond our control — that our well being or lack thereof is a result of environment, conditioning, biology, or institutional authority.

I would venture it to be a law of action that in order for outward acts to achieve their purpose, they must have their source in the inner recesses and identity of the self. Consider the metaphorical significance of what Ortega y Gasset has called the "great withdrawals into the self" that preceded the ministries of the more significant prophets of religion. As he observes: "It is no chance that all the great founders of religions preceded their apostolates by famous retreats. Buddha withdraws to the forest; Mahomet withdraws to his tent, and even there he withdraws from his tent by wrapping his head in his cloak; above all, Jesus goes apart into the desert for forty days."[52] Why are such retreats necessary? Are they not symbolic representations of an inner process each of us must carry out in order for our projects and social involvements to bear fruit? Do they not illustrate that for us to live and act in the world we must do so as if emerging or springing forth from a place that, if not outside the world of social relations, is at some partial remove from it — a dimension within the self?

The underlying principle of such retreats is the same: effective action has its basis not in what is external or superficial, but in the inner regions of the self. In cultivating inwardness, we are cultivating a basis from which to act and fashioning a self that may be invested and expressed in action. For this reason, it may be said that being fully present in our actions and in our lives is both a task and an achievement. Being present in, or fully in touch with, life is nothing less than acting on the basis of our choices and our identity as persons and engaging the world with some intensity. This is appropriately described as an achievement since to do it we must overcome obstacles such as the mental haze in which so much of everyday life is lived, the self-imposed unconsciousness and unreflectiveness of modern life, the instincts of security, conformity, and so on. Indeed, it is remarkable how many obstacles of this kind modern culture erects. At the same time we lament the absence of meaning in our private lives and the dehumanization of public life, we continue to judge the value of our actions by their capacity to bring approval, to prize security and material comfort over values of a more authentic kind. We continue as well to be herded together into a mass and treated as such by institutions of our own creation. We complain that our political rulers have "lost touch" and are all the same, but continue to elect them and quickly dismiss any whose views do not follow an established party line. Is it only our politicians who have lost touch?

53

Life as expansive vitality. But again the question confronts us: what is it with which we have lost touch? The answer appears to be life itself, yet what exactly does this mean? What is the "life" from which we are disconnected, and which we imagine certain others (such as artists, prophets, or children) to possess in abundance? Here we are dealing with a concept of no little ambiguity. If we may not catalogue exhaustively every one of its properties, we must at the very least offer an impressionistic account of the matter at hand.

In the most general terms, life may be conceived as a certain animating vitality arising from within which is inherently expansive, or which seeks of its own accord to expand and to expend itself in action. It is vital energy oriented toward a goal beyond mere survival or pleasure. Its essential aim is neither to endure nor to gratify itself, but to discharge itself. It achieves this through a series of life processes in which we all participate in one fashion or other. There are several points here that require elaboration.

First, life is a certain vital energy animating our outward movements and inner experience. It has often been given proper names: the "life force," "*élan vital*," and the "pleasure principle" are a few of the more widely known. Such proper names, in my view, serve no useful purpose, instead introducing unnecessary complications or outright errors when something that is inherently nebulous and intangible is transformed into a fixed metaphysical essence. Life is not thing-like or a stable substance that we can put under a microscope or whose metaphysical properties we could catalog. It is best described in impressionistic terms as a basic vitality or animating "spirit" — and where "spirit" is neither a mystical force nor a concrete entity of any sort, but remains an intangible. The vital energy of which life consists is closer to the order of physical nature and organic processes than to the order of metaphysics. As such, it is less something we hold in our hands than something that works through us. It is vital energy arising from within while directed toward a goal beyond the self, or beyond personal survival and pleasure. It seeks to discharge, or to expend, itself.

Nietzsche described this as the "will to power," where power refers not to domination over other persons but to the instinct to express or externalize the form of the self in one's environment.

That which possesses life possesses the will to discharge its strength and to affirm itself. Far from seeking a merely pleasurable or tensionless existence, it aims at a heightening of tension and at an overcoming of all that negates life. Above all, it is an exuberance that would express itself in both outward acts and inner integrity. That life is inherently expansive may be seen from the phenomena of growth and maturation. What has life grows and matures, not only in the sense that it gets older or larger, but that it seeks continual expansion. It develops a broader horizon of understanding and range of experience, it seeks a deeper involvement with the world and other persons, it refashions portions of the environment in its own likeness, while absorbing and learning more from its environment. That which not only lives but affirms life does not cease doing any of these things. What does not expand contracts, stiffens, and ultimately perishes.

Life is not something that we can bend to our will or order about. It works through us, emerging through our actions and passions, often in utter defiance of our will. It resists our choices, for instance, to stand still or to cease growing and expanding. Life is neither master nor slave to the will, but, when we live well, is its accomplice. It supplies the impetus for our chosen aims while having aims of its own. The alienation and despair we feel is often the price we pay for turning away from life and its imperative toward unceasing development.

54

"... *this flame, which is life*...."[53] Perhaps life would be best described not as a noun at all, but a verb — it is "living," after all, that we experience, something that we do, something in which we become caught up or that overtakes us. Living presses forward (life, as we say, "goes on"), emerging from within while striving to transcend the self. It is generated from the inside out and invariably culminates in the creation of something — an act, a word, an expression — beyond the agent who produces it. It gives birth to something that may take on a life of its own, quite apart from its creator or its creator's intention. Like a flame, it is in perpetual motion, change being its only absolute. Like a flame, it is most itself in reaching beyond itself.

55

The process of living. Life, for a tree, is nothing apart from a process by which elements extracted from the earth and the general environment are taken into itself, synthesized and transformed, culminating in the bearing of fruit — which itself is but a seed by which the same process can begin anew in a different form. The tree, for all we can discern, does not live "for the sake of" its fruit. Indeed, its only "for the sake of" is itself. Yet paradoxically inherent to this "for the sake of," co-mingling with its egoism as it were, is the seed that transcends it. Its life is not merely the servant of other lives to come; yet the process by which it lives leads by a logic of its own toward the creation of other life. It bears fruit and multiplies not as an act of duty, but as the most profound egoism — an egoism that in time will leave the ego itself in its wake.

56

Joie de vivre. The joy of life. We do not say "the despair of life." We despair over the circumstances of life. We do not despair of life.

57

Life and youth. It has always, I suspect, been an instinctive realization of the very young that for all the advantages of age, their elders have lost touch with something of vital importance, something with which children are intimately acquainted. They sense to their profound disappointment a certain absence of vitality, a dulling of the senses, that masks itself behind authority and adult seriousness. They sense this, moreover, not as a simple fact but as a betrayal. It is themselves their elders have betrayed, or even life itself. If an animal in the wild could speak, and if it could compare its way of life to that of its domesticated counterpart, I can only imagine it would pronounce a similar judgment to the judgment of children with respect to their elders: you have lost connection with that vital something that sustains us all; you have surrendered it by your own choice in exchange for security, ease, and in the case of human beings, power; you have become normalized and domesticated at the price of youthful exuberance or even honesty; you have lost even the awareness of having done so. The verdict of the child is often very harsh indeed, and at times it is accurate.

When Nietzsche sought to envision the sort of god that even he could believe in (skeptic that he was), he proposed: "I should believe only in a God who understood how to dance. And when I beheld my devil, I found him serious, thorough, profound, solemn: it was the Spirit of Gravity — through him all things are ruined."[54] When he contemplated the highest expression of life, he proposed the metaphor of the child at play. Here we find a thorough absorption in the present, in unselfconscious participation in action, and a love of one's fate. The child at play is not "merely playing," in the sense of acting frivolously or to no end. On the contrary, the child plays with a resolute purpose: it is to win, to outdo his or her companions, or to create something of unquestionable value.

What is it about childhood that so often prompts us to nostalgia? In some respects we quite idolize childhood and youth, including our own childhood. The golden age always lies in the distant past, but what is it about that period of life that invites nostalgia? The life of children is in many ways far from ideal. They are continually subject to authority and inhibited from acting as they wish. They live in a world that is by, for, and of the adult, and are often painfully aware of this. What is it that children do or feel that invokes such nostalgia? The answer is identified by both Nietzsche and Freud: children play, they are intensely and unself-consciously absorbed in the present; their actions demonstrate a spontaneity and honesty that is uncommon in the world of the adult which, as Freud put it, is governed by the "reality principle," while the world of the child is ruled by the "pleasure principle." What is the urge to return to childhood but the desire for play and the free expression of spontaneity — an escape from "the Spirit of Gravity" and the "reality principle"? It is the vibrancy and complete absorption in the present that we wish to regain and for which leisure is the nearest substitute. Yet even our leisure is more often a distraction than play or life itself. The capacity of the adult to become thoroughly absorbed in present activity without the unwelcome intervention of worldly concerns, still more to affirm a love of one's fate, is rare indeed.

58

Living and strategizing. There is a sense in which the art of living is the very opposite of the strategic mode of life so widely prevalent in modern times. For the latter all action is taken with an eye to gaining an advantage (often, but not always, at another's expense), all choices and relationships are means of "meeting needs" or getting what we want. Approaching life as if it were a kind of contest, perhaps a kinder, gentler form of war, produces a condition readily observable today in which our efforts to dominate the scene bear frustration, disconnection, and alienation as their consequences. It is a familiar truth that those who live by the sword die by the sword, that actions in general contain invitations for others or the universe at large to respond in kind, yet we frequently conduct ourselves as if we were unaware of this. In the end, every Goliath meets his David, every Napoleon meets his Waterloo. Our personal experience confirms this, even as we imagine that in our own case our actions might escape their natural consequences.

We often hear it asked why contemporary society seems to foster such advanced levels of anger, frustration, and alienation, evidence of which is visible every time we step outside our doors. While these are complex phenomena, I would venture that they are largely products of a way of life that is increasingly dominated by strategic ways of thinking and acting. The art of living is marked by a certain capacity for subtlety and silence, by a predilection for intangibles, all of which strategic ways of thinking relegate to the margins of life since they produce no immediate or tangible gain.

59

Life processes. If life is less something that we control or hold in our hands than something that works through us, it does so within life processes of several kinds. These are forms of action in which human beings invariably participate, but most often without explicit awareness. To live is to be already playing them out, to be in the midst of a current possessing a pace and direction of its own, yet which allows for creative negotiation. It is such processes that I have been speaking of throughout this chapter. To live as a human being is to understand oneself and one's world, to create meaning, fashion an identity, digest experiences, expand and incorporate elements of one's environment, stand out, express oneself, and participate in a general economy of life. Essentially, to live is to act and to choose, hence to exercise our freedom toward a set of conscious purposes.

The most fundamental opposition in human existence is not between life and death but between living and standing still. Dying is not the antithesis of living, but is one of life's processes, one that may itself demonstrate a profound affirmation of life, even exemplify life in an intensified form. Dying and grieving both belong to larger life processes, including several of those listed above. Both are tasks that call upon us to understand the meaning of a life that is now at an end, to contemplate who that individual was and what lessons their life imparts, and to digest fully the significance of what has taken place. Both crucially involve the capacities of freedom, understanding and self-understanding, responsibility and choice — including the choice of life or death in the face of suffering.

It is not death, then, that stands in opposition to life, but standing still, motionlessness, or a refusal of participation in life processes. I have spoken of life as something — an expansive vitality — that, in a sense, works through us while it is also a process in which we freely participate. Are these two statements contradictory? Can life, or living, be simultaneously something that we do and something that happens to us? Can we be both active and passive with respect to life? Here I would suggest that the verb "living" contains both an active and passive connotation, and in a way that avoids contradiction. Living, like "participating," is essentially an act — something that we freely do — yet one that takes place within a context of environment and circumstances that we do not choose. Metaphorically, to live is to find oneself in a river with its own source, direction, and current, yet to be capable of negotiating it in order to reach a destination of one's choice. Here one's freedom is not unlimited, but it is sufficient for the purposes of human life. A skilled navigator does not merely follow the current wherever it leads — which would not properly be conceived as navigation at all, but drifting — but knows he must heed the law of the sea in order to arrive at his destination. Metaphors often become clichés, as this one certainly is, but when they do it is generally on account of their ability to express something fundamental about human existence.

"Participation" is a term that appropriately expresses how human beings stand toward life and the general circumstances in which we find ourselves. To participate is to act with a purpose of one's own, but it is simultaneously to play a part in a larger process which one does not altogether control. Participation is intermediate between submission and domination, and contains elements of both activity and passivity. To participate effectively in most any endeavor, one must do so on a conscious basis. One must be attentive to the dynamic or spirit inherent to that endeavor and to one's role in ensuring its continuation or success. By the same token, the failure of participation may take the form either of refusing to play one's role or of insisting on a dominant position.

It is characteristic of modern life, however, to seek optimal control over outward circumstances, rather than to participate in this sense of the term. When it is security that we seek, we must optimize control over our circumstances, including the persons and objects in our environment. We must transform them as much as possible into objects of our will. Accordingly, modern science and technology seek a kind of mastery over the natural and social worlds. Social institutions plan, regulate, and administer much of human life rather than allow us the freedom to make choices and to accept responsibility for their consequences. The dynamic openness of life is restricted in the fear that we shall fail to gain a level of security and material comfort.

It is therefore fitting to ask whether it is really life that we seek, or whether it is the security that arrests life. The preoccupation with control and security is not a means of living well, but a respite from the task of living itself.

60

Organic processes. In speaking of life as participation in processes in which we are all continually engaged, I have placed some emphasis on human freedom in relation to our environment and circumstances. We live by our capacities of understanding and existential decision, yet at the same time we are organic beings whose mode of life is conditioned by natural, organic processes of various kinds. We are accustomed to speaking of human beings as "the rational animal," yet it is hardly reason alone by which we live. The human being is, after all, a physical organism, not a disembodied intellect. Our physicality is in many ways as central to our mode of life as our more cerebral qualities.

To live is to do so in connection with vital energies which have their source in organic processes. It is typical of these processes to possess a fundamentally rhythmic structure. As participants in nature, we move within rhythms of birth and death, growth and decay, sleep and wakefulness, expansion and contraction, desire and aversion, and many other natural polarities. Much of the business of living consists in negotiating these tensions or in the essential to and fro of opposing forces. While tension is something that we generally seek to avoid insofar as possible, the ideal of a tension-free existence is not a human existence at all, nor is it a possible existence for any living organism. Only in death are we released from the antagonism of forces in nature.

We have long been accustomed to thinking of our intellectual and psychological life as made up in large part of a play of oppositions. There is good and evil, truth and falsehood, love and hate, attraction and repulsion, and a thousand other oppositions that we must resolve in some more or less satisfactory way. Conflict and ambivalence belong to the human condition not as an accidental circumstance, but as a necessary consequence of our participation in a natural order. As conscious, rational beings, we can tolerate no contradictions, while at the level of the unconscious we can and do. As Freud so often had occasion to observe, human consciousness and reason float on a surface of contradictory instincts which are never perfectly resolved or held in control.

Ultimately, it is the rhythm of life and death, the passing of the generations, that forms the basic structure of human existence. The many other organic processes and oppositions all move in accordance with this most fundamental rhythm of nature. If life were a piece of music (and what is music but a metaphorical representation of life?), the opposition of life and death would constitute its basic rhythm, while the various melodies and harmonies would consist of oppositions of desire and satisfaction, passion and aversion, good and evil, night and day, the changing of the seasons, and so on. It would be music of no little intricacy and complexity, with layers of melody and rhythm, abrupt changes and sudden departures within a more or less coherent arrangement. It would also be something that we are swept up into, and in which we may become carried away. A rhythm is something that we move in accordance with, which defies both standing still and attempts to dominate or control it. We no more control it than it controls us. We move, or dance, to a rhythm in a fashion that it does not dictate, yet move to it we must.

So it is in the case of all of nature's processes in which we participate. We stand toward nature and our own physicality in much the way we stand toward our culture: we stand entirely within it, yet in a manner that it does not and cannot command. Nature enjoins us to grow and to expand, but it does not say in what direction. It compels us to exercise our faculties of perception and emotion, but it does not say how. We are not always free; there is genuine necessity in nature, and we forget this at our peril. But the art of coping with necessity is among the surest marks of our freedom.

61

Spirituality and self-realization. The human self is embedded in both a social and a natural environment. Its life takes form within these environments and is in part fashioned by them. Self-realization is achieved only against the background that they form. We "stand out" not in a vacuum, but against a general context that surrounds us. Yet we also stand within a larger universe of earth and sky, atoms and planets, a general cosmos of matter and energy in which life is embedded. Life reverberates with that from which it emerges, the general play of forces that govern the astronomically large and the infinitesimally small. Life processes have their counterparts in cosmic processes, making it possible for human beings to identify in some fashion with the larger universe in which we live.

The time would seem to have passed when we could subscribe wholeheartedly to the spiritualities of former ages. Ancient religions of both the West and the East have suffered the fate that is inevitable when authentic spirituality gives rise to mass movements, institutions, and creeds in mutual competition. Little credibility remained, for instance, of the Christian "religion of love" after the brutality of the religious wars, the crusades and witch hunts, the internal dissension and splintering of the movement during and following the Reformation, and the centuries of intolerance that this religion long inspired. What the Christian movement did not destroy of Christian spirituality, the combined efforts of modern science and philosophical skepticism accomplished by shattering one by one the dogmas of the ancient creed. Ultimately, however, it was less modern science and philosophy — outsiders of religion that they are — that brought about the veritable demise of the Christian religion than the internal disintegration of the tradition itself. Modern efforts toward its rehabilitation inevitably fail to capture that which gave Christianity its birth. Between the spirituality of Jesus and the frantic, dogmatizing fundamentalism of our times, little resemblance can be seen.

If a return to the past is not a genuine option — and when is it? — then we require a different kind of spirituality from the religions of old. The desire for an alternative spirituality is widespread in modern culture, as evidenced by the emergence of the human potential movement, new age and feminist spiritualities, witchcraft, and so on. While I do not propose to defend any of these, or for that matter to criticize them, what is remarkable is the tendency they sometimes demonstrate to articulate and practice a form of spirituality that is without dogma, institutional authority, and the trappings of a creed. If any possibility of authentic spirituality exists in the modern world, a spirituality that requires no sacrifice of intellectual honesty, it is to be found in a spiritual practice that is devoid of unquestionable truths, solemn institutions, and mass movements. It would be an affair of inwardness and attunement to the processes in the universe that mirror the fundamental processes of life.

Whatever spirituality is, in its innermost essence, it involves at the very least a kind of attunement or orientation toward the universe, one that fastens upon those processes and forces that reverberate deeply within the self. There is one sense, at least, in which we are not alone in the universe. While the gods may have fled, the universe nonetheless heeds principles that are not without counterparts in the world of human affairs and within the individual self. The aspiration of human life to expand and to perceive the form of the self reflected in the universe sometimes succeeds. When it does, it has been made possible by forms of awareness that are attuned simultaneously to what is deep within and what is visible in the farthest reaches of perception. There is more under the sun than simple matter in motion, causes and effects, and mechanical predictabilities. There is the sublime and the beautiful, the metaphorical, and the unknowable. There is spiritual and aesthetic elegance, cosmic processes echoing life processes, and forces of nature that reflect the play of human relations.

If authentic spirituality remains a possibility for modern life, I suspect it would assume the form of a spirituality of self-realization. In being an affair of inwardness, it would defy all efforts to transform it into a mass movement, to institutionalize it, or to burden it with a creed. It would have no need for dogmas that could be placed in opposition to those of rival traditions, but would attend to the general edification and liberation of human potential. It would be a spirituality of the body, of this earth and this life, with no superstructure of authority and mystification. Whether such a spirituality is beginning to assume lasting form, or whether spirituality in all its forms is in its final death throes, is too soon to tell. What may be foreseen — indeed, what was foreseen well over a century ago when Nietzsche announced the "death of God" — is the demise of ancient mythologies which for centuries burdened the human spirit under the guise of spirituality.

62

Spirituality and the "axial age." The "axial age" is the name Jaspers gives to the period in ancient history during which the founders of the great world religions and the earliest philosophers lived. Its principal figures include Socrates, Plato, Zoroaster, Gautama Buddha, and Jesus, among others. Social theorist Lewis Mumford proposed the intriguing hypothesis that this general period of ancient history was witnessing a reaction against pervasive and often dehumanizing structures of "civilization" and bureaucratization. It was a reaction that assumed a spiritual form, or indeed a variety of spiritual forms, which gave rise to traditions of belief. During the span of a few centuries (beginning in the neighborhood of 600 B.C.), humankind underwent a profound shift in both ethical values and spirituality, a kind of spiritual maturation which led to the establishing of Zoroastrianism, Buddhism, Christianity, and the other world religions.

If it is fair to say that during this general period of human history mankind experienced something like a maturation or "development" of the species that took on an ethical and spiritual dimension, then one question arises: what made this possible? How does it come to pass — if indeed it does — that whole cultures "mature," as we speak of individuals maturing over the course of a lifetime? Is it triggered by any particular set of conditions?

If Mumford is correct (and I would emphasize the "if," since we are speaking here in terms of broad impressions, if not outright speculation) in his impression of the axial age as witnessing a pervasive reaction against impersonal and dehumanizing structures of "civilization," this speaks to the capacity of an entire culture to take a step forward in its spiritual maturation out of collective opposition to conditions or forces widely experienced by members of that culture as stultifying to the human spirit. Indeed, it is noteworthy how many advances in history arise out of opposition to institutions or ways of thinking that keep the human spirit in a condition of servility. Advances are then greeted not only as improvements, but as liberations that alter the course of history.

Our own age is often described as one of dehumanizing bureaucratization and rationalization, one in which social life becomes an "iron cage" of institutional authority, technological rationality, and impersonal forces which the individual is at a loss to understand much less to control. With equal frequency, the modern age is described as a period of transition, although to what we do not know. Perhaps these two descriptions are not accidentally related. We cannot describe history before it happens, but it is an intriguing possibility that modern culture is entering not only an "information age," but an age of heightened spiritualization very different from the religious spiritualities of the past. We may hope, at any rate, that this might be the case. We might hope that an age of information will not deteriorate into one of meaningless facts and dumbfounding technology, but that it might be accompanied by an attunement toward the inner dimensions of the self and the larger universe from which life emerges.

CHAPTER 5

LIVING IN THE FACE OF DEATH

63

Living and choosing. We all live by our choices. Even when we are unaware of this, as we often are, our personal history is a history of choices we have made in response to the unchangeable "givens" of our existence. It is a history of decisions that we either arrived at autonomously or delivered over to others to make for us, of actions taken voluntarily or out of conformity to public opinion, and of values and beliefs adopted in full awareness of their significance to our lives or merely gone along with unreflectively. In either case, it is our choice whether to take our decisions into our own hands or to surrender this responsibility to others.

To live by our choices is to accept responsibility for their consequences. It is not to expect to be rescued from these consequences, or from ourselves, but to live in the realization that our lives are our own. What does it mean to say that our lives are our own, that the choices by which we live are properly ours to make, that we must base them on our own understanding, and that we may not expect to be rescued from their consequences? It is not to say that each of us is alone in the universe, as we certainly are not, but that the responsibility for our individual existence belongs to us as individuals.

Among the choices by which we live, the most profound is the choice of life or death in the face of suffering. It is a choice that we would sooner not make, and the ways of the world would lead us to believe that it is not ours to make — that the matter is for an unseen power to decide, for medical professionals, loved ones, public opinion, or most anyone but the individual. Much the same applies to the other momentous decisions each of us faces: the beliefs and values that fundamentally orient our lives, the social roles and lifestyle we adopt, the customs and traditions we take up or leave behind. Consciousness is itself a choice, whether we shall actively contemplate and digest the experiences that make up our lives or cultivate unconsciousness. When life itself compels us to attend to the fundamental issues of our lives, as it does in the encounter with death, it is essentially toward a re-examination of our choices that we are compelled. Most of all, we are compelled either to live in the face of death or to evade life as it is. Here there is no third option: to turn our back on death is nothing else but to turn our back on life, with all the consequences that follow from this. By the same token, to encounter life authentically is to live in the face of death.

64

Affirming our existence. Yet what is it to live in the face of death? What manner of life is this, if it is not merely one spent in a perpetual state of morbid brooding? Must we assume an air of existential angst in order to be connected with life? The obvious answer is that we do not. Living in the face of death, in short, is living with the capacity to say yes to our existence as it in fact is.

Nietzsche expressed a similar idea in his notion of the "eternal return." He asks us to imagine that our lives will occur again, indeed an infinite number of times, and exactly as we have lived them. Would we greet the news that we shall relive each of our experiences infinitely as a cause for celebration, he asks, or as the most disagreeable fate we could imagine? Our answer will reveal something of significance about the way we lead our lives and about our capacity to affirm our existence as it is. The kind of individual Nietzsche admired loves his or her fate and would welcome the news of life's eternal recurrence as a liberation. Most of us would be somewhat more reserved on the issue.

To perceive the human condition and one's own life as they really are, and to be able to say yes to both (anyway) is no small achievement. To be conscious of our limitations, of the contingency of all things, and of the fact of our mortality — without the need to look away or to lie — is fundamental to the task of being human. If we are a species that lives by our consciousness, then we must become conscious of reality in both its lighter and darker aspects, transforming what we can and accepting what we cannot. Among the unchangeable realities of human existence is the inevitability of one's personal death. To affirm that existence, then, is to accept this inevitability — perhaps even to affirm death itself.

We affirm death as we affirm life, by imposing meaning on the meaningless through an act of will. As philosopher James Carse observes: "[I]n all great systems of thought the agency of death is alien and hostile, but it is *also* an invitation to new life. What first appears as the willful destroyer of meaning in human existence comes to be seen as the very point of access to a more durable meaning, one that can embrace all forms of meaninglessness possible."[55] It is one of the ironies of human life that to live well we must cultivate an awareness of the tragic and the sorrowful, that if we cannot look in the face of tragedy our existence has an inevitable falsity about it. We cannot impose meaning upon our experiences without recognizing their inherent meaninglessness. We cannot create values without comprehending that the objects of our desire are without value in themselves. Similarly, we cannot affirm our lives as a totality without affirming our death. Looking upon the tragic dimension of life makes possible a more complete self-affirmation, one that is without qualifications or contradictions. It is a self-affirmation that says yes to life in spite of its darker aspects — or even because of them.

65

Keeping death before our imagination. One of the soundest recommendations regarding our attitude toward death was expressed in the sixteenth century by philosopher Michel de Montaigne, who wrote: "Let us strip away [death's] strangeness, engage with it, accustom ourselves to it, having nothing more frequently in mind than death. At every instant let us have it before our imagination, in all its guises. At the stumbling of a horse, the fall of a stone, the slightest prick of a pin, let us think to ourself: Well, and what if *this* were finally death? And thereupon let us be strong of heart, strong of will.

Amidst feasts and pleasures we should always keep in mind the remembrance of our condition, never let ourselves be so carried away
with pleasures that our memory fails to remind us how many are the
ways that our happiness can fall prey to death, how many are the
ways she threatens us. . . . Forethought of death is forethought of
freedom. Who has learned to die, has unlearned servility."[56] In this
concise passage Montaigne suggests that we keep the possibility of
our personal death regularly before our minds not in order to
dampen our happiness — something there could be no point in doing — but precisely to create a more robust happiness, one firmly
rooted in the process of living.

There is a freedom and an exuberance that come from the realization that we can live in the face of death, that we can overcome
death's power to terrify by overcoming its foreignness. We do not
fear what we know; we neither fear in the deepest recesses of our
being nor hold in the highest reverence that with which we are intimately acquainted. Familiarity breeds contempt, where contempt
means not disdain but an absence of strong feeling of any kind. In
the case of death, it is unlikely in the extreme that we shall ever be
without powerful emotions toward our own death or the death of
persons close to us, nor is this an aim worth seeking. It is only by
lying about death convincingly that we could ever eliminate profound feelings of sorrow and loss. An aim that is worth striving for,
however, is to eliminate the terror that makes such lies appear necessary. We achieve this in much the same way that we overcome
other fears, by reducing it to an object of everyday familiarity, anticipating it as a possibility every day of our lives, imagining that it
might confront us immediately.

Living in the face of death means living in the realization that death is more than a merely abstract possibility. It is our most concrete possibility, one that puts an end to all other possibilities. It is also the most certain of inevitabilities. Keeping this before our minds not only allows us to accept what we cannot change, but, as Montaigne observed, it also has a liberating effect. It frees us from common evasions and illusions regarding death, which keep us in a condition of self-chosen immaturity and alienation from life. It makes possible a more robust and whole-hearted affirmation of life. We do not say yes to life by hedging it with a thousand qualifications. To affirm life is to affirm one's own life as a totality, not only its more pleasant aspects.

When we refuse to regard death as an ever-present possibility, we invite self-deception and the consequences of self-deception. Tolstoy described this mercilessly in *The Death of Ivan Ilych.* After a lifetime of preoccupation with gaining outward respectability and social position, Ilych, sensing his imminent death, continued to repress that knowledge, only for death to force itself upon his attention at every moment: "And what was worst of all was that It drew his attention to itself not in order to make him take some action but only that he should look at It, look it straight in the face: look at it and without doing anything, suffer inexpressibly. And to save himself from this condition Ivan Ilych looked for consolations — new screens — and new screens were found and for a while seemed to save him, but then they immediately fell to pieces or rather became transparent, as if It penetrated them and nothing could veil It."[57] This is the phenomenon Freud called "the return of the repressed": what we repress returns to consciousness with redoubled urgency and in a form we do not wish. The freedom that is gained in keeping the possibility of death before our imagination is the freedom that accompanies intellectual honesty. It is a freedom that affirms life, and is opposed to the servility that comes with fear.

66

Life as an end in itself. To live is to be oriented toward a future. While we live in the present, and draw upon the past, human life is inherently future-oriented in the sense that our choices and actions are undertaken with an anticipation of what they will bring about. It is for the sake of its future consequences that much of our present assumes the form that it does.

If it is characteristic of human existence to be future-oriented in this sense — that particular endeavors are undertaken for the sake of an expected future — does this entail that life itself is merely a means to an end? It is necessary to raise this question explicitly in light of how often in human history life has been conceived as a means to an end, particularly where the end is an afterlife believed to be superior to this earthly existence. That the purpose of this life lies beyond it in a promised land of religion, or a superior rebirth, has been the dominant view of human life since ancient times. So much so, in fact, that life has traditionally been conceived as having no meaning whatever apart from that to which it is a means.

The decline of religious worldviews in modern times prompts us to revisit this question. It is, after all, a question that is second to none in both philosophical and practical importance. My own view on the matter is that life is never a means to an end beyond life. Just as one's own life is never a mere means to the life or happiness of another person, neither is it merely a means or preparation for a life to come. Indeed, if it were possible to blaspheme this life and this world, it would be by regarding the worth of either as contingent on something beyond itself, and in particular by conceiving of life as a dress rehearsal for a life beyond this life. It is only the individual occurrences of a life that may be means to ends beyond themselves, not that life as a totality.

This holds not only in the case of human life, but indeed for all life. It is often said that an organism in nature exists in order to fulfill its "biological function," and thereby to perpetuate the species to which it belongs, or more broadly in order to serve the larger ecosystem in which it lives. Yet do we really know this to be the case? What we can know by observing a living organism's behavior is that it desires to reproduce, to care for its offspring, to survive, and to provide for its various needs. What we do not know — what in principle we are prevented from knowing — is the larger "what for?" of its existence. All that we are capable of knowing, for instance, about a cat's purpose in living is that it desires to live, and to live as nothing other than a cat. Whether it could care less about its "biological function," its species, or the ecosystem we shall never know.

We simply have no reason to believe that life — any life — is ever a mere means to an end — any end — beyond that life. What we do know is that when an individual life is regarded as a means to the ends of a god, a nation, a movement, or another individual, that life suffers a profound loss of dignity that is not restored in the event that it succeeds as a means. That the highest purpose of living consists in something beyond life itself is a doctrine that has assumed many forms in history, all of which are profoundly anti-life.

67

Living without immortality. We do not know, we shall never know with certainty, whether there is a life beyond this life. Nor do we know whether a deity resembling the Biblical God, or any other form of divinity, exists. Philosopher Blaise Pascal argued in the seventeenth century that while we possess no convincing evidence of the Biblical God's existence, or of the existence of an afterlife, we should choose to believe both propositions anyway. His famous "wager" proposed the view that while we do not know either of these claims to be true, it is better to believe both in the event that they are. If the Biblical story is true, he reasoned, we are better off believing in it and leading our lives accordingly, since we stand to gain an eternal reward for doing so, and eternal damnation for doing the reverse. If the Biblical story is untrue, we still lose relatively little in thinking it true. It is unlikely that many have been won over to the Christian way of life by Pascal's wager, yet it is not uncommon to hold that just in case there is an afterlife, we had better live as if there is. While this view is not often formulated explicitly, it is often held implicitly by those who prefer not to spend too much time contemplating such matters. It is sometimes held as well by moderate skeptics of religion, who prefer to hedge their skepticism in case they turn out to be mistaken.

For my part, I would propose the directly opposite view. Even if there is an afterlife, it is better to live as if there is not. I say this for several reasons. First, intellectual honesty demands that we suspend judgment in the case of a belief or proposition that is without compelling evidence in its favor (or compelling evidence against it), particularly when that belief carries far-reaching implications for how we live. There is no belief that carries more such implications than the belief in an afterlife. Second, as I have remarked above, if the notion of "blasphemy" holds any meaning outside of a religious context, then it is a profound blasphemy to this life to regard it — still more to live it — as if it were a preparation for something else. Indeed, even if there were an afterlife, it would not follow that this life must therefore be a preparation for it, hence a means to an end. Third, if there is an afterlife, we can do little better than guess whether it bears any resemblance to any of the competing accounts of it that have been offered by the various world religions. Here we are in the land of speculation, and we shall not break out of it in this life.

Finally, to live as if there is not an afterlife is to live in the face of death, and indeed to live truly — where "truly" means with some intensity, passionately, and in the present. There is a tendency in believing in the afterlife to live in some measure for the future, to look forward to a day when we shall receive our just reward and all will be as it ought, and for this reason to lessen our commitment to this life. Were I a lawyer presenting my case before a judge while believing that the present trial will be appealed, and that the deciding trial is still in the future, I can imagine a voice whispering in my ear: "Do not trouble yourself with your arguments and all your details and fine points; this trial is merely a rehearsal for the trial that is to come. Do not worry if the next ruling does not go in your favor; it will have no bearing on the final outcome."

When we live in the expectation of an eternal reward, and under the threat of damnation, our lives become a little less our own, and become instead something that is on loan or held on probation. Ultimately it belongs to an authority to whom we must answer rather than answering to ourselves, rather than being something that we must realize in our own fashion. To live means to live without appeal, without the fantasy that one day an unseen authority will render all as it should be. Why, after all, ought we to labor to make our lives and this world as we imagine they ought to be if in the end divine authority, quite apart from our efforts, is certain to set all matters to rights?

68

The limits of knowledge. It is one of the tragic realities of human existence that we often encounter the limits of what is knowable where the desire for knowledge is most urgent. In the encounter with death there is nothing we desire more than to know what happens to the human being after death, whether we may believe in some form of personal survival in an afterlife of whatever description, or whether we must renounce the belief in immortality as unprovable. I have argued that whatever the facts of the matter turn out to be, it is better for the purposes of this life to live as if there is no afterlife. In all contemplation of death, it is ultimately life — this life — that we are brought round to contemplating, and which is the ultimate object of our concern. But having said this, the question obstinately refuses to go away: is there a life beyond this life?

Here we are brought up against a wall. The only intellectually responsible reply to the question is that not one of us knows with anything approaching certainty. We have intuitions, hunches, anticipations, even strongly held beliefs, but we cannot know. If there is an afterlife we shall know it with certainty when we die, but not sooner. For all the tales that we tell, all the testimony regarding past lives, near-death experiences, and the rest — all of which fascinate the imagination as nothing else — still we encounter a wall through which no light penetrates. On this issue, the most exacting research will not be able to disentangle the reality from the profound psychological investment we all have — including researchers themselves — in the nature of that reality, or from the emotional imperative to bend reality to our wishes. Living in the face of death means living in the face of mystery, and accepting the mystery for what it is. The will to live itself rails against mystery and eagerly clings to whatever elements of hope and purported certainty present themselves, but the sobering truth of the matter remains the same. We shall not know prior to death whether there is or is not any form of personal survival beyond death.

69

Metaphorical survival. Apart from the question of literal survival beyond death is the issue of metaphorical survival. Symbolically, we do survive death in a variety of forms, and from the standpoint of this life — and what other standpoint do we occupy? — these forms are of no less importance than literal survival in an afterlife. We all know that there is metaphorical survival in the lives of our children and grandchildren, in the memory of persons close to us, in the achievements and projects that we leave behind, and in the lessons that our lives impart. Beyond this, there is an interconnectedness of life that ties us to future generations, just as we are profoundly connected to prior generations. There is the cycle of birth and death, the continuation of life processes which both precede and survive us.

It is a common expression that, when someone close to us dies, a part of ourselves dies with them. Metaphorically, this is true. Our identity as individual selves is profoundly linked with the identity and being of particular persons in our lives, those "significant others" who have a profound bearing on who we are. As Augustine wrote: "Someone once spoke of his friend as 'the half of my own soul.' I agree, for I felt that my soul and that of my friend had been one soul in two bodies. So I had a horror of going on living, because I did not wish to live on as a half-person. And perhaps, too, that was the reason why I was afraid to die — lest he, whom I had loved so much, should die completely."[58]

By the same token, if we are profoundly interconnected with particular others and with larger processes of life, then a part of oneself does survive in the continuation of that from which one's own existence emerged, and in the continuation as well of those persons with whom our life was intimately linked.

70

Hope and mystery. Many who are accustomed to belief in an afterlife will find all talk of metaphorical survival a pale comfort. There is no shortage in our culture, or in most any culture, of persons and institutions anxious to provide consolation in any form to those facing death or its aftermath. Many of these would say just about anything in the effort to comfort and console, and too often at the price of surrendering all reason. There is no topic on which we are quicker to abandon our wits than death and the afterlife. There is a need, not for fresh efforts in this direction, but for a measure of intellectual honesty to identify that which may and may not be known as well as that for which we may hope.

Prior to our personal death, we shall not know definitively whether there is life beyond death. Nor should we expect investigation into the psychological experiences of the dying or near-dead to discover anything conclusive, or even reasonably probable, on the issue. In the present age of science, we are uncomfortable with mystery — not the mystery of what scientific investigation has yet to turn up, but the full-fledged mystery of what it will never discover, or what is genuinely unknowable. Yet here we find the ultimate mystery of human existence, a mystery that is universal yet at the same time profoundly personal. In the encounter with mystery there is a certain tactfulness, even solemnity, that forbids all rash claims to certainty. It forbids equally the religious claim to knowledge of an afterlife and the claim to knowledge in the opposite direction. We are, in modern culture, on the verge of forgetting that we need not, and cannot, know everything. Nor is it imperative that we hold opinions on all subjects. On this subject in particular, there is no belief that has any greater claim to our allegiance than another.

If in the encounter with mystery there is neither certainty nor even reasonable belief, there remains the imperative of hope. The voice of hope is the voice of life itself, a universal affirmation of life in the face of death. It is the obstinate refusal to allow death the final say, a protest of one's whole being against the annihilation of life. The basic movement of life is toward more life — toward unceasing expansion and the anticipation of a future. It is a movement toward exuberance and self-affirmation, one that compels us to hope for some manner of personal survival beyond death, even as wisdom disciplines that hope.

Philosopher Miguel de Unamuno writes: "In the most secret recess of the spirit of the man who believes that death will put an end to his personal consciousness and even to his memory forever, in that inner recess, even without his knowing it perhaps, a shadow hovers, a vague shadow lurks, a shadow of the shadow of uncertainty, and, while he tells himself: 'There's nothing for it but to live this passing life, for there is no other!' at the same time he hears, in this most secret recess, his own doubt murmur: 'Who knows?. . .' He is not sure he hears aright, but he hears. Likewise, in some recess of the soul of the true believer who has faith in a future life, a muffled voice, the voice of uncertainty, murmurs in his spirit's ear: 'Who knows? . . .'"[59]

At the conclusion of Dostoyevsky's *The Brothers Karamazov*, a group of children poses the question to Alyosha Karamazov whether they shall one day meet again the friend whose funeral they have just attended: "Karamazov, can it be true, as our religion claims, that we shall all rise from the dead, come back to life, and meet again, Ilyusha too?" To this Alyosha replies: "We shall certainly rise and we shall certainly all meet again and tell each other happily and joyfully everything that has happened to us." Who among us is not moved to the depths of our being by the anticipation that "we shall meet again" in an existence beyond death? This is the obstinacy of hope. It is the instinct of life working through us that compels us to anticipate that which we cannot know.

Notes

1. Sigmund Freud, "Thoughts for the Times on War and Death" in *Death: Philosophical Soundings*, ed. Herbert Fingarette (Chicago: Open Court, 1996), p. 150.

2. Leo Tolstoy, *The Death of Ivan Ilych* in *Great Short Works of Leo Tolstoy*, ed. John Bayley (New York: Harper and Row, 1967), p. 280.

3. Freud, "Thoughts for the Times on War and Death," p. 150.

4. Fyodor Dostoyevsky, *Notes From Underground* (New York: Bantam Books, 1981), p. 152.

5. See Martin Heidegger, *Being and Time* (New York: Harper and Row, 1962), section 40.

6. Herbert Fingarette makes the same observation as follows: "To try to contemplate the meaning of my death is in fact to reveal to myself the meaning of my life." Fingarette, *Death: Philosophical Soundings*, p. 5.

7. See Elisabeth Kubler-Ross, *On Death and Dying* (New York: Macmillan Publishing, 1969).

8. Edwin S. Shneidman, *Deaths of Man* (Baltimore: Penguin Books, 1974), p. 7.

9. Friedrich Nietzsche, *Beyond Good and Evil: Prelude to a Philosophy of the Future* (New York: Vintage Books, 1989), section 157.

10. Rollo May, *Man's Search for Himself* (New York: Signet, 1967), pp. 148-9.

11. Shneidman, *Deaths of Man*, p. 87.

12. Henry Murray, "What Should Psychologists Do About Psychoanalysis?" Quoted in Shneidmen, *Deaths of Man*, p. 58.

13. Nietzsche, *Thus Spoke Zarathustra: A Book for Everyone and No One* (New York: Penguin Books, 1985), p. 97.

14. Tolstoy, *The Death of Ivan Ilych*, p. 286.

15. Herbert Marcuse, "The Ideology of Death" in *The Meaning of Death*, ed. Herman Feifel (New York: McGraw-Hill, 1959), p. 66.

16. See Paul Fairfield, *Moral Selfhood in the Liberal Tradition: The Politics of Individuality* (Toronto: University of Toronto Press, 2000).

17. Paul Tillich, "The Eternal Now" in *The Meaning of Death*, ed. Herman Feifel (New York: McGraw-Hill, 1959), p. 30.

18. May, *Man's Search for Himself*, p. 29.

19. Nietzsche, *On the Genealogy of Morals* (New York: Vintage Books, 1956), p. 229.

20. Viktor Frankl, *Man's Search for Meaning* (New York: Washington Square Press, 1985), p. 152.

21. See *ibid.*, p. 128.

22. May, *Man's Search for Himself*, p. 22.

23. Karl Jaspers, *Man in the Modern Age* (New York: Doubleday Anchor Books, 1957), p. 42.

24. Vaclav Havel, *Living in Truth*, ed. Jan Vladislav (Boston: Faber and Faber, 1989), p. 54.

25. Jose Ortega y Gasset, *Man and People* (New York: W. W. Norton, 1963), p. 99.

26. Quoted in *Dying: A Book of Comfort*, ed. Pat McNees (New York: Warner Books, 1996), p. 39.

27. Plato, *Phaedo* in *The Collected Dialogues of Plato*, ed. Edith Hamilton and Huntington Cairns (Princeton: Princeton University Press, 1961), p. 64a.

28. *Ibid.*, 67e.

29. Albert Camus, *The Myth of Sisyphus and Other Essays* (New York: Vin-

tage Books, 1955), p. 3.

30. Eugene Halton, *Bereft of Reason: On the Decline of Social Thought and Prospects for its Renewal* (Chicago: University of Chicago Press, 1995), p. 42.

31. Ortega y Gasset, *Man and People*, p. 55.

32. C. G. Prado, *The Last Choice: Preemptive Suicide in Advanced Age* (Westport: Praeger, 1998), p. 2.

33. *Ibid.*, p. 75.

34. David Hume, *Essays: Moral, Political and Literary* (Oxford: Oxford University Press, 1963), p. 595.

35. *Ibid.*, p. 615.

36. Nietzsche, *Thus Spoke Zarathustra*, 98.

37. *Ibid.*, p. 97.

38. Prado, *The Last Choice*, pp. 114-5.

39. *Ibid.*, p. 67.

40. Emile Durkheim, *Suicide* (New York: The Free Press, 1951), p. 145.

41. *Ibid.*, p. 208.

42. *Ibid.*, p. 217.

43. *Ibid.*, p. 373.

44. *Ibid.*, p. 209.

45. Tillich, "The Eternal Now," pp. 34-5.

46. Frankl, *Man's Search for Meaning*, p. 121.

47. Ortega y Gasset, *Man and People*, p. 25.

48. Frankl, *Man's Search for Meaning*, pp. 126-7.

49. Nietzsche, *Thus Spoke Zarathustra*, p. 161.

50. Nietzsche, *The Gay Science* (New York: Vintage Books, 1974), section 290.

51. Nietzsche, *Thus Spoke Zarathustra*, p. 120.

52. Ortega y Gasset, *Man and People*, p. 35.

53. Gabriel Marcel, *Homo Viator* (New York: Harper and Row, 1962), p. 43.

53. Nietzsche, *Thus Spoke Zarathustra*, p. 68.

54. James Carse, *Death and Existence: A Conceptual History of Human Mortality* (New York: John Wiley and Sons, 1980), p. 9.

55. Michel de Montaigne, "To Philosophize is to Learn to Die" in *Death: Philosophical Soundings*, ed. Herbert Fingarette (Chicago: Open Court, 1996), p. 166-7.

56. Tolstoy, *The Death of Ivan Ilych*, pp. 281-2.

57. Quoted in *Dying: A Book of Comfort*, ed. McNees, p. 172.

58. Quoted in *The Oxford Book of Death*, ed. D. J. Enright (Oxford: Oxford University Press, 1983), p. 159.

59. Dostoyevsky, *The Brothers Karamazov* (New York: Bantam Books, 1981), p. 936.

In the same collection from Algora Publishing:

Time & Ego. Judeo-Christian Egotheism and the Anglo-Saxon Industrial Revolution
— by Claudiu A. Secara

A Passion for Democracy: Benjamin Constant
— by Tzvetan Todorov

The Tyranny of Pleasure
— by Jean-Claude Guillebaud

Coping with Freedom. Reflections on Ephemeral Happiness
— by Chantal Thomas

Refounding the World: A Western Testament
— by Jean-Claude Guillebaud

Mystic Chords. Mysticism and Psychology in Popular Music
— by Manish Soni